2020

Editor
Sidney Gottlieb

Editorial Advisory Board
Richard Allen   Thomas L. Leitch
James Naremore   David Sterritt
Michael Walker

Founding Editor
Christopher Brookhouse

Editorial Associate
Renata Jackson

Cover Design
Deborah Dutko

We evaluate manuscripts for the *Hitchcock Annual* throughout the year. Send any correspondence by mail to Sidney Gottlieb, Department of Communication and Media Studies, Sacred Heart University, 5151 Park Avenue, Fairfield, Connecticut 06825. Send submissions by e-mail to spgottlieb@aol.com

We invite articles on all aspects of Hitchcock's life, works, and influence, and encourage a variety of critical approaches, methods, and viewpoints. For all submissions, follow the guidelines of the *Chicago Manual of Style*, using full notes rather than works cited format. We prefer submissions by e-mail, in any standard word processing format, which makes it easier to circulate essays for editorial review. The responsibility for securing any permissions required for publishing material in the essay rests with the author. Illustrations may be included, but as separate JPG or TIF files rather than as part of the text file. Decision time is normally within three months. The submission of an essay indicates your commitment to publish it, if accepted, in the *Hitchcock Annual*, and that it is not simultaneously under consideration for publication elsewhere.

For all orders, including back issues, contact Columbia University Press, 61 West 62nd Street, New York, NY 10023; www.columbia/edu/cu/cup

The *Hitchcock Annual* is indexed in the *Film Literature Index* and *MLA International Bibliography*.

Columbia University Press   *New York*

Columbia University Press
Publishers Since 1893
New York   Chichester, West Sussex

Copyright © 2021 Sidney Gottlieb/*Hitchcock Annual*

ISBN 978-0-231-19957-5 (pbk. : alk. paper)
ISSN 1062-5518

∞

Columbia University Press books are printed on
permanent and durable acid-free paper.
This book is printed on paper with recycled content.

Printed in the United States of America

p 10 9 8 7 6 5 4 3 2 1

References to Internet Web sites (URLs) were accurate at the
time of writing. Neither the editors nor Columbia University
Press are responsible for URLs that may have expired or
changed since the manuscript was prepared

HITCHCOCK ANNUAL
2020

MICHAEL WALKER

Suspicion *Revisited*

Very few Hitchcock films have produced as many articles over the years as *Suspicion* (1941). The reasons for this are well-known: Hitchcock had enormous problems with the film's ending, and did indeed give different accounts of these problems at different times. Critical research through the various archives has not just revealed the extent of these problems—shown in the dizzying number of script amendments, which continued up to the final days of filming—but also suggests a confusion of intentions right through to the final released version of the film. But even the ending as it stands has been criticized by many ever since the film's release.

In 1998, I made my own contribution to this critical debate in an article, "Can Cary Grant Be a Murderer?," written for *Unexplored Hitchcock*, an anthology which was never published. But whereas most articles written for that book, by myself and others, did subsequently find a home, often in *Hitchcock Annual*, this particular article was comprehensively upstaged by Bill Krohn's "Ambivalence (*Suspicion*)," published in *Hitchcock Annual* 2002-03.[1] Krohn's research, conducted in the U.S., was superior to my own, conducted in the U.K., and I shelved my article.

Krohn's article did not, however, bring a halt to the flow of material on *Suspicion*. Krohn had already rehearsed his article on the MacGuffin website in 2001,[2] and a 2002 article by Rick Worland in *Cinema Journal* with further information about the previews of the film prompted Krohn to return to the website in 2003 to publish yet more ideas about the film's ending(s).[3] A chapter by Patrick Faubert in *Hitchcock and Adaptation* (2014) summarizes the previous debates about the endings, but also introduces new material in the form of the RKO scripts of the source novel, Francis Iles's *Before the Fact* (1932), written *before* Hitchcock was involved in the project.[4] In an essay in *A Companion to Alfred Hitchcock* (2014), Tania Modleski makes some highly pertinent observations about the significance of the two female scriptwriters on the film—Joan Harrison and Alma Reville—and the film's female point of view.[5] I would in particular like to add my support to Modleski's criticisms of perhaps the most substantial article on *Suspicion*, that by Mark Crispin Miller.[6] Miller is patronizing towards the "woman's film," and seeks to rescue *Suspicion* from so impoverished a genre. Modleski elegantly draws attention to the bias of his observations.

However, despite all this material, many of the points in my original article still seem valid. Accordingly, I would like to look once more at *Suspicion*, considering my earlier thoughts in the light of these more recent contributions.

*   *   *   *   *   *

There were obvious problems from the beginning with a film adaptation of *Before the Fact*. The novel concerns a woman who gradually realizes that her husband not only married her for her money, but intends to kill her, and she finally submits and allows him to do so. Such a plot in itself would have been almost impossible to film, but other details make matters worse. The novel covers over ten years of the marriage, during which time Lina also discovers that Johnnie has been having affairs with dozens of women, including her best friend; that he impregnated the maid in the first year of the marriage; and, to hasten Lina's inheritance, later planned and brought about the death of her father (by daring him into a fatal over-exertion while drunk). Twice she attempts to leave him, but her love for him draws her back. Then Johnnie's friend Beaky dies in Paris (as in the film, but here Johnnie is unambiguously responsible) and, having conned Lina into insuring her life (he will also inherit her considerable fortune),

Johnnie starts to plan how to kill her. As Lina slowly faces up to this, she enters into a fever of masochistic suffering, awaiting the death she knows could occur at any moment. Her discovery that she's pregnant merely provides her with a rationalization for her submission to death: "Johnnie must not be allowed to reproduce himself."[7] Realizing that Johnnie intends to use the "untraceable poison" her crime novelist friend Isobel Sedbusk has discovered, Lina ensures that he will get away with her murder by writing a suicide note to Isobel and then drinking the poisoned milk. As she's dying, she's moved to tears by the thought that Johnnie will miss her.

Quite obviously, *Before the Fact* is a feminist's nightmare. The weakness of the heroine also presents enormous difficulties for a film adaptation: the idea of a woman allowing her husband to murder her out of "love" for him is simply too perverse. In the light of this, one of the solutions that Hitchcock came up with makes sense. According to Donald Spoto, RKO gave Hitchcock the go-ahead because his plan was that "he, Alma and Joan would revise the story by making the husband's deeds the fictions in the mind of a neurotically suspicious woman."[8]

Spoto is keen to emphasize this, because, as he points out, Hitchcock's later story, as told to Truffaut, was that he had wanted to follow the novel more closely: Johnnie (Cary Grant) would bring Lina (Joan Fontaine) the poisoned milk, Lina would write a letter to her mother incriminating him, then drink the milk; Johnnie would post the letter.[9] In support of this, Ken Mogg among others has pointed out just how many references there are to letters and stamps throughout the movie, preparing the way for this ending.[10] Even Hitchcock's cameo shows him posting a letter. But such an ending was impossible: the producers would have insisted, in Hitchcock's words to Truffaut, that "Cary Grant cannot be a murderer."[11]

In fact, there is a much stronger reason for the impossibility of this ending. It's not so much that Cary Grant could not play a murderer, but that Joan Fontaine as wife could not be killed, especially if she herself colluded in her murder. Spoto speaks of a sub-plot being written in to discredit her by having her commit adultery, and misrepresents the nature of her death by referring to it simply as suicide, but it's still unprecedented that such a figure be killed off in such a manner at the end of a classical Hollywood film. *Sorry, Wrong Number* (Anatole Litvak, 1948) illustrates the nature of the problem: in order for an audience to accept its ending—the wife being murdered at the husband's albeit reluctant instigation—the wife is made unsympathetic throughout the film. Lina, by contrast, is our identification figure from the opening scene. An audience would inevitably reject an ending in which she was killed.

To the best of my knowledge, no one has pointed this out. But Alma—and, surely, Joan Harrison—would have known. They would equally have known that, if Lina thinks the milk is poisoned, she must not drink it. In fact, this point was amply demonstrated at the two previews, where the version screened showed Lina drinking what she thinks is poisoned milk. It turns out she is mistaken, but Johnnie is so shocked at the revelation of Lina's suspicions that he promises to reform. However, when Lina drank the milk, the preview audience roared with laughter.[12] Nevertheless, this did not stop Hitchcock, who shot another ending (not, apparently, previewed) in which Lina only drinks some of the milk, and it is when Johnnie feeds the rest to the dog that she realizes it is not poisoned.[13] Here Johnnie's vow to reform is less convincing, and Lina's expression tells the audience she doesn't believe him. Krohn argues that this ending, keeping in the detail that had made the audiences laugh, but "topping it with the moment when Johnnie feeds the milk to the dog, which would have provoked an even bigger laugh, this time from the whole audience, [puts] the joke . . . on the scoffers who couldn't believe that a woman could love her husband so much that she'd drink milk she believed to be poisoned." He calls this the "gutsy choice."[14]

I completely disagree: it would have been the nasty choice. Indeed, some of the preview cards were absolutely insistent: Lina must not drink the milk.[15] Making a sympathetic heroine as masochistic as that would be terrible box office.

The ending of the film as it stands may be unconvincing, but at least here Lina does not drink the milk. But that leaves the question of whether or not it was poisoned unresolved. Accordingly, any "explanation" of what has been going on must necessarily be clouded with uncertainty. I see no reason why we should believe the suddenly introduced notion that Johnnie was interested in Isobel's untraceable poison because he was contemplating suicide. As Richard Allen has suggested, the film's last shots are deeply ambiguous. Johnnie is now driving Lina home; their backs are to the camera: "As the romantic music swells, Johnnie coils his arm around Lina in a romantic embrace. But is this a romantic embrace or the snake-like coil of death?"[16]

Others have made a similar point. In his Jesuitical reading of Hitchcock, Neil P. Hurley comments: "More than one woman in the audience has felt that *she* would not choose to return home with such a husband. . . . One has the eerie sense that there could be a next time, that Johnnie is looking for the opportune moment to commit murder."[17] As Krohn points out, even Hitchcock has suggested as much, when he responded to a question by Peter Bogdanovich about the ending by saying that "it would have been better if I'd shown them both driving and he'd just look back over his shoulder regretfully—because he didn't push her over. Missed his chance."[18] This would in fact have been a terrible ending, but it does indicate that Hitchcock continued to think of Johnnie as a murderer.

There is in fact one critic who assumes that Johnnie is a murderer throughout. In his review of the film in *Cahiers du Cinéma*, Pascal Kane simply ignores the "compromises" and writes about the film as if it were much the same as the novel, i.e., he reads the film in line with Hitchcock's observation to Truffaut that he wanted Johnnie to be a murderer. Even so, the only real evidence that Kane produces for such a reading is that "[Lina] is always behind with each of Johnnie's lies, and this is so systematic that her death is ultimately "programmed" by the end of the film."[19]

Figure 1

Because of the ambiguity of the ending, it is only through a careful consideration of the earlier events that we can see what the film is really implying. I would like to start with the opening scene.

Suspicion begins in darkness; background noise tells us we're on a train. A man's voice is heard, "I beg your pardon. Was that your leg?" In the darkness resulting from the train going into a tunnel, Johnnie has magically found his way into Lina's carriage. It's precisely as if she has conjured him up. Moreover, the Lina we see here, in a tightly buttoned coat, reading a book on child psychology, is the sort of young woman we can imagine might fantasize that an interesting young man would find his way to her compartment (fig. 1). In fact, Johnnie seems at first to be presumptuous: to make up the money he owes the conductor (Billy Bevan), he cheekily invades her handbag for a stamp. But, as he settles down to sleep off a hangover (fig. 2), Lina is startled to discover a photograph of him accompanied by a Mrs. Newsham (Isabel Jeans) in the *Illustrated London News* she now opens. Johnnie is a glamorous celebrity.

Figure 2

In the next scene, her re-evaluation here is matched by his. As horses, hounds, and riders gather for a hunt, a photographer (Clyde Cook) is trying to get Johnnie and his two female companions (one, significantly, Mrs. Newsham) to pose for a photograph. However, Johnnie keeps being distracted, and one distraction is his sight of Lina calming a restive horse. His comment, "It can't be the same girl" could be seen as an echo of her thought as she identifies him in the *Illustrated London News*. In the train, wearing lace-up shoes, she appeared to him prim and dowdy; now she appears in a markedly more attractive light: stylish, even dashing, and a member of the hunt (fig. 3).

As the narrative returns to Lina there is, again, a sense of her conjuring Johnnie up. She sits in the living room of her family's spacious Tudor house, reading a book. Behind her is a large window (fig. 4). Some neighbours, Mrs. Barham (Violet Shelton) and her two daughters, appear at the window and distract her. They have arrived to see her because the man accompanying them insisted. As they stand in the doorway, Johnnie steps forward. He wants Lina to come with them to church.

Figure 3

Here a sense of the oneiric is aided by the window behind Lina: it's like a screen onto which her fantasies could be projected. Architecturally, the door is within the window (in the long shot across the room to Lina, we probably don't realize that there is a door), so that Johnnie actually steps through this "screen space." And now, as Lina goes off to change for church, he discovers for himself that she has been thinking of him. In her book, he finds the torn out photograph of himself and Mrs. Newsham.

These opening scenes suggest an underlying pattern: there is a sense in which events have an element of fantasy, as though Lina is projecting herself into a "romantic" narrative. From this point on, virtually the whole film is from Lina's point of view, in the sense that she is in almost every scene and events within the scenes are shaded to suggest her perceptions. Speaking of the fairy-tale elements to movies which center on a heroine and her emotional journey, Marina Warner comments:

> The gateway to fantasy (and especially erotic fantasy) when translated to screen is opened in sleep or dreams. It is through fantasy, through the uses of

Figure 4

enchantment, that she achieves her passage from one
state to another, that she manages to tame or
otherwise come to terms with the Beast. . . . The
dreaming heroine, often considered a mere passive
victim, shouldn't be underestimated. There is a sense
that she is voyaging, and that the film we are
watching . . . emerge[s] from her fantasy.[20]

However, as Warner stresses, the "fantasies" these
heroines experience can be fraught with difficulties. Johnnie
distracts Lina from church and takes her for a walk. Hitchcock
cuts to a distance shot of the two on a hilltop, involved in
some sort of struggle. Indeed, Lina is struggling so hard to
resist whatever Johnnie is doing to her that she loses her coat,
hat, and handbag (fig. 5). Jarring chords on the soundtrack
suggest threat. In a closer shot, Johnnie, still holding both
Lina's wrists, mocks her panic: "What did you think I was
trying to do—kill you?" Asserting that she thought he was
trying to kiss her, he claims he was really trying to fix her
hair. The ludicrousness of this as an explanation for the
quite violent scene we have just witnessed is part of the

Figure 5

point. In effect, this can be seen as the founding moment of their relationship: as though the ambiguity of what Johnnie wants to do to her is, for Lina, a constant source of disturbance and excitement. That she experiences the ambiguity as also exciting is implied by her return to the hilltop during the period when she is anxiously waiting for Johnnie to contact her.

When, on the hilltop, Johnnie really does then try to kiss Lina, she resists. Hitchcock here shows his cheeky way with Freudian symbols by having her signal her refusal by closing her handbag. But, as Johnnie walks her home, from outside her house Lina overhears her parents discussing her: her father (Cedric Hardwicke) declares that she'll never marry, and her mother (Dame May Whitty) tends to agree, saying "she is rather spinsterish." Immediately Lina turns to kiss Johnnie. As she then enters the house, Hitchcock pans to frame a "phallic" newel head in the foreground (fig. 6). Lina is aroused by Johnnie's sexual allure, but equally there is a sense of desperation in her kiss, a desperation which suggests her dread of remaining a spinster.

Figure 6

Although since he became a major star, Cary Grant had appeared mainly in comedies, he was undoubtedly a highly romantic figure. It is this romantic persona, and the sexual promise that it carries, that leads Lina to pursue Johnnie. This leads into the familiar narrative of the heroine seeking to win the reckless and promiscuous hero as husband; to tame him into domesticity. We note that it is Johnnie's subsequent history of his sexual conquests—his joking reference to having once counted up to seventy-three previous girlfriends—that first prompts Lina to declare her love for him. But Lina is responding purely to the surface allure: she has no idea what Johnnie is really like. Her father's view, that Johnnie is the black sheep of his family ("Pity he's turned out so wild"), is by no means discredited.

After their first kiss, Johnnie simply disappears, and Lina becomes increasingly despairing of seeing him again. On the evening of the hunt ball, which she had fantasized going to with Johnnie, she furthers the fairy-tale subtext when she declares to her mother, like a failed Cinderella, "I'm not going to the ball." But then a telegram from Johnnie arrives, and Lina is immediately transformed into a glamorous Cinderella.

Figure 7

She goes to the ball, Johnnie arrives and sweeps her away from it, and by the end of the evening they have decided to marry. Both know that General McLaidlaw will disapprove, so they ask permission of his portrait (fig. 7).

The speed with which this occurs suggests Johnnie's impulsiveness. In the novel, Johnnie marries Lina opportunistically, knowing her family has money which will one day be hers, but Johnnie in the film seems carried away by romantic enthusiasm. He is no less irresponsible financially than his prototype, but he seems less calculating. In these early scenes, the casting of Cary Grant lightens the role; he lacks the heartless ruthlessness of the novel's Johnnie.

It is not until after the honeymoon that Lina discovers Johnnie has no money. As he is showing her the lavish house he has rented and decorated, she asks him if he can afford it, but he keeps interrupting her. Then a letter arrives asking for the return of £1000 Johnnie borrowed for the honeymoon and the house. Only now does Johnnie admit he's penniless, saying he has been broke all his life. He assumes that Lina can pay his debts; when he learns she can't, he suggests she approach her father. But General McLaidlaw so disapproves

Figure 8

of Johnnie that his wedding gift serves to mock Johnnie's hopes for money: he sends them a pair of antique chairs. Lina proposes that Johnnie find work, but he promptly turns this suggestion into a joke. Nevertheless, the scene ends with Johnnie, pressured by the General (on the phone), showing Lina a letter from his cousin Captain Melbeck (Leo G. Carroll) offering him a job.

However, Lina still has to realize that Johnnie does not work—he expects to be kept. He also gambles at the races. Lina learns about the latter when Johnnie's friend Beaky (Nigel Bruce) comes to stay, saying he ran into Johnnie at Newbury Races. When Lina notices that the antique chairs are now missing, Beaky knows at once that Johnnie has sold them to pay his racing debts; he likewise tells Lina gleefully that Johnnie will of course lie about this. Beaky is right, but at this stage Lina accepts Johnnie's lie. In one of the very few scenes in the film outside her consciousness, Johnnie signals to Beaky over her head that he should have kept quiet (fig. 8). It is only later, when Lina subsequently sees the chairs for sale in an antiques shop window, that she realises Beaky had been right. But again Johnnie placates her, returning home with presents for everyone, claiming he has won £2000 at the races. He has also bought back the chairs.

We will learn later that Johnnie did not win £2000 at the races; he stole it from Melbeck. But the striking point is that, having stolen the money, he promptly spent it or, at least, most of it. In the novel, where Johnnie hasn't the slightest compunction about stealing, and will soon move on to murdering for money, such recklessness is understandable. But in the film, again, it suggests Johnnie's impulsiveness.

An old school friend, Beaky serves to highlight both Johnnie's immaturity and his potency.[21] On the one hand, he and Johnnie behave like overgrown schoolboys together; on the other, Beaky is an emasculated buffoon: the present Johnnie gives him, mockingly, is a walking stick. Beaky also has a life-threatening medical condition, which means he has to be careful about drinking. Johnnie knows about this, but allows him here to drink brandy, whereupon Beaky is promptly seized by the sort of coughing fit that suggests imminent collapse. Another matter is that Beaky is drinking to toast Johnnie's vow to stop gambling: "The last bet, old bean." His fit thus also serves as a comment on the spuriousness of Johnnie's vow.

For a time Johnnie pretends to work, leaving each day for what Lina assumes is the job with Melbeck. But when Lina encounters Mrs. Newsham in the village, the latter is eager to pass on the news that she saw Johnnie at the races. Lina goes to Captain Melbeck to check, and discovers that Johnnie was fired six weeks ago for embezzling £2000.

Melbeck actually comments to Lina, rhetorically, "How does he get away with it?" Moreover, Johnnie's ability always to "get away with it" extends to Lina. Having discovered that he is a thief, she decides to leave him. In the first scene set in the bedroom, she writes him a farewell letter, but then tears it up. At that moment, in the first of what will become a series of sinister entrances, Johnnie appears behind her in the background (fig. 9). Seeing that she's upset, he asks, "Then you've heard?" Thinking that he means about the embezzlement, she says yes. But he means about the death of her father, and shows her the telegram. The death of her

Figure 9

father thus functions implicitly as both Lina's punishment for thinking of leaving Johnnie and her excuse to embrace him tearfully: to cry because, as in the novel, she is too weak to leave him.

Although, unlike in the novel, there is no hint here that Johnnie hastened General McLaidlaw's death, he was certainly hoping to benefit from it, anticipating that her father would leave Lina some money in his will. But, in an overt demonstration of his disapproval of the marriage, the General declines, leaving her only his portrait. Johnnie himself knows why the General does this: in another scene outside Lina's consciousness, he goes into the study after the will-reading and ironically toasts the portrait, '"You win, old boy" (fig. 10).

This scene is also significant because of Johnnie's apparent deference to the General. In the other two moments where we see Johnnie do something unknown to Lina—mouthing a protest to Beaky; later telling Melbeck over the phone he expects to repay him soon—he is behaving just as we would expect: seeking to control or placate the older man and so keep his dishonesty a secret from Lina. But, from the General,

Figure 10

he seemingly accepts defeat. However, it could be that the General's decision to leave Lina any money simply raises the stakes. In the car drive home after the funeral, Johnnie lets slip an uncompleted thought which begins "If you were to die first, I . . . ."

In fact, Johnnie's next attempt to find someone who will support him involves Beaky. Beaky is rich, and Johnnie persuades him into an ambitious clifftop real estate plan, a plan which Lina quickly realizes Beaky does not understand. But Johnnie overhears her probing Beaky about this and becomes very angry. It is at this point that, as a husband, he starts to become more sinister: not just a happy-go-lucky spendthrift but someone who turns aggressive when his dubious plans are threatened with exposure.

Johnnie makes his displeasure known to Lina as they go upstairs to change for dinner. After his outburst, they walk side by side in silence (fig. 11). This is the first time that one of the film's most striking visual motifs—a pattern of shadows through a skylight over the hallway that suggests a spider's web—becomes prominent. Although the spider's-web imagery in the hallway is in fact present from the opening

Figure 11

scene in the house, at first it is a background presence. Now it has become heightened—as though intensified by Johnnie's anger, an anger prompted by Lina's growing suspicion that he is after Beaky's money.

The next day, in the second of his sinister entrances, Johnnie suddenly appears in the foreground before Lina in the garden, startling her (fig. 12). He announces that he will abandon the real estate plan. We suspect that this is because Lina is now suspicious of his motives, but he cannot admit this, so he improvises a series of reasons for his decision, such as perhaps the land isn't suitable, or he doesn't want to risk Beaky's money, or he's too lazy. But Lina's concern, after his anger last night, is whether or not he still loves her? Here Johnnie reassures her with practiced skill, but as he walks away she still has a questioning, uncertain look on her face.

There follows a remarkable dissolve, from Lina's face to the letters "DOUB" (fig. 13). Johnnie, Lina and Beaky are playing a game of anagrams, but this association—the word formed will be "DOUBT"—subliminally alerts the audience to the way Lina's mind now is working. As the game continues, Johnnie tells Beaky he wants him to come to the clifftop site

Figure 12

Figure 13

tomorrow so that he can show him why he wants to abandon
the plan. As Lina forms the word "MURDER," Beaky comments
that, if he had "er" he could make "murderer." This causes
Lina to link the comment with Johnnie and to fantasize

Figure 14

Johnnie pushing Beaky off the clifftop: a fantasy which Hitchcock shows in superimposition over her shocked face (fig. 14). Robin Wood speaks of this as depicting the workings of her unconscious: "subconsciously, she *wants* [Johnnie] to be a murderer."[22] But the moment also has other connotations. First, Lina may well secretly want to get rid of Beaky, who keeps moving in to stay with them, encouraging Johnnie's childish irresponsibility through his own amusement at its various forms. Her resentment of Beaky may also be unconsciously exacerbated by a link the film sets up: he is presented, through a number of associations, like an emasculated version of her father. Although Beaky's, significantly, is rarely lit, both men are pipe smokers. Beaky first arrives to stay on the day the antique chairs vanish, as though, symbolically, he is replacing them. And the second time he comes to stay is immediately after the General's death. In other words, Beaky's fantasized death may be seen, on two counts, as a projection of Lina's own unconscious wish. Second, Lina's fantasy could also be an expression of her own death drive: her masochistic fear of being killed by Johnnie. Her dramatic faint which follows the fantasy makes her seem like the victim.

The condensation of material in Lina's fantasy is typically Freudian, another example of the psychoanalytical richness in Hitchcock's work. It hints at the masochistic repressed in Lina and, if the connection between Beaky and the General is valid, at her unconscious desire for patricide. But it is marked, nevertheless, as a fantasy. In particular, subsequent events seemingly show that Lina's fears were groundless: not only did Johnnie not push Beaky off the cliff, but he saved Beaky's life when the latter was stupidly backing the car towards the end of the cliff. But (a) this incident is straight from the novel, where Lina realizes that Johnnie only saved Beaky's life here because he hadn't yet got his hands on Beaky's money,[23] and (b) the incident also makes perfect sense as a last minute failure of nerve. Beaky had protested that there was no need for him to visit the clifftop, but Johnnie had insisted. It's as though Johnnie took him there to kill him, manoeuvred him into backing the car towards the edge, and then suddenly couldn't go through with "the accident." In other words, even the apparent contradiction of Lina's fantasy of Johnnie as a murderer is ambiguous.

* * * * * *

But is it possible to argue that Johnnie's apparent murderousness is only "in the mind of a neurotically suspicious woman"? Lina marries Johnnie not only to assert her own sexuality, but in defiance of her father. We might therefore expect her to fear some kind of punishment: perhaps seeing Johnnie as a murderer fits this. Lina never escapes the influence of her father: he himself ensures this, first through the gift of the chairs (which stand in for the parents who would have occupied them); then his portrait, which both Lina and Johnnie address as though talking to the General. The latter is particularly significant, because Lina describes the study where it hangs in the family mansion as her "favorite room," in effect characterizing herself as "Daddy's girl." Both the chairs and the portrait symbolize the

Figure 15

General's presence as a superego figure, a presence which is introduced into the marital home.

Moreover, each time an older man enters the narrative, he provides information which reinforces the General's negative view of Johnnie. Beaky enlightens Lina about the fate of the chairs and Johnnie's propensity to tell lies. Melbeck informs her that Johnnie stole £2000. And when the third such figure, Inspector Hodgson (Lumsden Hare), comes with a colleague to inform Lina of Beaky's death in Paris, Hitchcock suddenly reintroduces the General's portrait, which appears in the shots with Lina as she reads a newspaper report of the death (fig. 15). From the inspector, Lina hears the details: Beaky died after drinking an excessive amount of brandy — apparently as a result of a bet with another Englishman, who promptly disappeared. The reintroduction of the General's portrait here emphasizes his superego power: after the policemen have gone, Lina is sufficiently worried that Johnnie might have been the man with Beaky that she feels obliged to protest to the portrait that he wasn't.

Figure 16

Because almost all the events are from Lina's point of view, Hitchcock is nevertheless able to sustain the ambiguity over whether or not Johnnie is a murderer. This takes us back to the spider's-web pattern of shadows. The pattern is particularly emphasized in this scene with the police: we see it when they arrive (fig. 16) and then immediately after they have left (fig. 17). Robin Wood comments on the latter:

> We see Joan Fontaine, now certain her suspicions are justified, standing in a black dress before a window whose framework casts around her a shadow of a huge web. She is feeling herself the victim, the fly caught in the trap. But the image suddenly gives us the truth—she is in reality the spider, fattening herself on her suspicions in the center of the web she has herself spun; or she is both spider and fly at once, victim of her own trap.[24]

Setting aside the trivial mistake about the window, this locates the origin of the spider's web with Lina: she is the spider. An alternative reading has been supplied by Richard Allen:

Figure 17

Lina's fears about the marriage are expressed through the *mise-en-scène* of the family home where the hallway doubles as a gigantic spider's web, with Johnnie the predatory spider at its centre. . . . It is . . . the positive reflection of her unconscious; that is, an unacknowledged desire to be stalked and captured. Yet the spider's web also reflects a reality— Johnnie is a predator, and portends the deaths that are to follow.[25]

The weakness of this argument is that, unlike Robin Wood's, it lacks a precise image on which to focus. However, as I argued with respect to Figure 11, there are indeed images which suggest that it is Johnnie rather than Lina who expressionistically heightens the spider's web. That is, although we may read Lina in Figure 17 as trapped in a web of her own suspicions, the suspicions themselves are well-founded. It is the information brought by the police that produces these two spider's-web images, and the information—about Beaky's death—is indeed suspicious.

Figure 18

After the police have left, all the evidence does in fact point to Johnnie's guilt. First, Lina phones and learns that Johnnie left the Hogarth Club in London the day before (and so could have gone to Paris); when he gets back home and phones the inspector, he lies about his whereabouts. Second, Johnnie's return home here is visualized as his third sinister entrance: he appears, shadowed, in the doorway (fig. 18), then stands over Lina—who presses herself back fearfully in an armchair—in a composition which suggests intimidation (fig. 19). When Lina tells him that the police wondered if he could help them identify the man who was with Beaky, he doesn't answer. When she says she told the police about the real estate corporation with Beaky, Johnnie says "I wish you'd left all that to me." His attitude suggests a concern that Lina has told the police something incriminating—the whole scene moves close to the one in Hitchcock's *Dial M for Murder* (1953), in which Tony (Ray Milland) seeks to disguise his own responsibility in the attempted murder of his wife Margot (Grace Kelly) by instructing her what to say to the police about the incident. Third, Johnnie arrives home here carrying the latest novel by Isobel Sedbusk, *Murder on the*

Figure 19

Footbridge, which, as Isobel (Auriol Lee) points out to Lina, includes the sort of "murder by staging an accident" that would fit Beaky's death. Fourth, Isobel also tells Lina that the "brandy thing" was not new, and that her copy of the book detailing the real-life case which made use of it for murder, *The Trial of Richard Palmer*, has been borrowed by Johnnie. Fifth, Lina finds this book not on the shelves, but "hidden" in a drawer, and inside it a letter to Melbeck pleading for more time to repay the £2000. These accumulated details actually go beyond the evidence Lina uncovers in the novel. It would seem that Hitchcock was determined to make Johnnie appear guilty.

At the same time, such an accumulation of incriminating evidence is in itself suspicious. In particular, why would Johnnie "hide" *The Trial of Richard Palmer* and leave inside an unsealed, unsent and compromising letter? It's as though these were intended for Lina to find. Here the film becomes even more difficult to decode. If it were just a question of the letter, we might see Johnnie's leaving it in the book as a Freudian slip, like the torn-out photograph Lina leaves in her book at the beginning: unconsciously, she wanted him to know she was attracted to him; unconsciously, he wants her to know he's in trouble. But such an explanation ignores the (inculpating) subject matter of the book. Moreover, the letter refers to a "scheme" which "did not come off," but adds "I'm sure I can find some other way" of repaying the stolen money. As Lina reads this, the phone rings. As though signalling what "some other way" might mean, the call is from an insurance company which has just written to Johnnie in answer to a query he made.

An important point about the first and third of Johnnie's sinister entrances is that these are scenes where, in the novel, he has just committed a murder. The scenes are not *from* the novel. There the deaths of both General McLaidlaw and Beaky are not followed by a scene in which Johnnie returns home.[26] But it's as though Hitchcock filmed these entrances with the novel at the back of his mind: Johnnie seems sinister because that's how Hitchcock felt about him—he is returning home *like* a murderer.

Moreover, by the time of the third such entrance, Lina herself would seem to have the same feelings. As Johnnie stands over her, he says (of Beaky), "Next to you, I loved him more than anybody in the world." Lina, cowering in the armchair, repeats, with almost tremulous fearfulness: "Next to me?" Her response suggests that she is thinking of herself as Johnnie's next victim.

That Johnnie is making enquiries of an insurance company furthers Lina's suspicions. The next morning, there are in fact letters from two insurance companies. Still in bed, Johnnie reads them surreptitiously, casting quick glances towards Lina (fig. 20). But he then slips them into his jacket pocket, not noticing that Lina witnesses this through a mirror. When Johnnie is out of the room, she is able to read at least one of the letters. Again, the contents are incriminating, stating that Johnnie cannot borrow against a policy, but only receive payment in the event of his wife's death. When Johnnie returns to the room, he comments on Lina's shivering. Implicitly, she is shivering with fear.

Figure 20

After this, Johnnie's behavior does in fact become increasingly sinister and threatening. The couple attend a dinner at Isobel's, where he shows great interest in a reference to an untraceable poison. At the end of the scene, Isobel declares that Johnnie couldn't commit murder, but, as he responds "No, I don't believe I could," he looks at Lina with an expression that turns very menacing just before the fadeout (fig. 21). Back home, as Johnnie bolts the door and reminds Lina that the cook and the maid are away, he seems to be amused at her obvious unease: as she hesitates at the foot of the stairs, he takes her hand to lead her upstairs as one would a fearful child. This is also a scene in which the spider's-web shadows are much in evidence. As they reach the bedroom, again Johnnie comments on Lina's shivering. In fact, she is so frightened that she asks him to sleep in his dressing-room. Far from reacting sympathetically, he at once turns nasty. Then, as he leaves, Lina collapses (a trace of her pregnancy at this stage in the novel?), which puts her into bed and under his ambiguously solicitous care.

Figure 21

There is a sense here that Johnnie is becoming sadistic, another trace of Johnnie in the novel. But we now also see complementary hints of Lina's masochism. When Lina awakes in bed, both Johnnie and Isobel are at her bedside. Left alone with Isobel, Lina learns that Johnnie has managed to worm the name of the untraceable poison out of her. Hitchcock films this with the camera on Lina, and two of her reactions to Isobel's story are very suggestive. First, as Isobel asks, "Have you ever been able to deny Johnnie anything?," Lina responds, breathily, "Never." Then, as Isobel finishes her account, Lina sinks back against the pillow, asking "Is whatever it is painful?" As she does this, and as Isobel replies, "Not in the least. In fact, I should think it would be a most pleasant death," Lina registers an almost erotic response, as if in masochistic submission at the thought of her own murder (fig. 22). In the next scene, Johnnie brings her the milk.

The shot of Johnnie carrying the milk upstairs, deep within the darkened hallway and the spider's-web shadows, the milk itself glowing from the light bulb Hitchcock placed in the glass, is the most famous image in the whole of *Suspicion*,

Figure 22

Figure 23

endlessly repeated in articles on, or just references to, the film (fig. 23). This is the culmination of the mystery, or threat, at the heart of the film: is Johnnie simply bringing Lina her night-time milk, or is he delivering the poison that is intended to kill her?

In fact, it is possible to see this image as the end point of a series of shadowed/barred images of Johnnie and Lina throughout the film. In Figure 1, there is a bar across Lina as she looks at Johnnie which, in her later point-of-view shot in Figure 2, is elaborated into a network of bars around Johnnie. Indeed, the bars here suggest the first signs of the spider's web. It is only after Johnnie has been identified as a celebrity that he visualized in this manner, as though the attraction of his glamorousness in itself signals danger. And so, there is from the beginning a textual hint that the meeting of this couple will lead them into a shadowed world. This is taken further when Lina enters her parents' house after first kissing Johnnie: in Figure 6, the hallway has a network of shadows on the walls, a much stronger anticipation of the spider's web. Here the patterning is overtly linked with Lina's desire. The shadow imagery then modulates through all the shots in the couple's home which include the spider's-web effect. It is apparent that the effect is, strictly speaking, expressionist, since its intensity is tied to Lina's feelings about Johnnie and it is no less prevalent at night—when the outside source would necessarily be the moon—as during the day.

As Johnnie leaves the milk, he says "Goodnight, Lina." This is highly significant, since on only one other occasion does he call her Lina: during the car drive after her father's funeral, when we have the first suggestion that Johnnie is thinking about Lina's possible death. At other times, he either calls her darling or, more often, by the nickname he has bestowed on her: Monkeyface. Now, this is from the novel, but it is—at least to modern ears—insultingly disparaging. It's as though Johnnie can only feel affection for Lina when he patronizes her, and calling her Monkeyface is part of this. As he delivers the milk, which the logic of the situation suggests is indeed poisoned, his calling her Lina connotes coldness and finality: he won't be seeing her again.

*   *   *   *   *   *

The "compromise" ending that follows keeps the darker implications of the story alive. Lina has not drunk the milk, but she is leaving to stay with her mother. Johnnie insists on

Figure 24

driving her. The events during the car drive along the clifftop road are highly suspicious: not only is Johnnie driving far too fast, but the car has suddenly developed a dodgy door, which does indeed spring open, exposing Lina to a life-threatening fall. But, instead of stopping, Johnnie continues to drive at a breakneck speed, while making an ambiguous lunge either across or towards Lina. At the very least, his actions are suspect.

One bizarre detail here is the crocheted hat that Lina wears over her hair; it's a Rosie the Riveter factory-style hairnet, which not only makes her look grotesque, but is quite inappropriate in class terms (fig. 24). The net comes off in the frenzy of the ensuing scene; I can only assume that was its main purpose. A link may then be drawn with the hilltop scene during Lina and Johnnie's first walk, with its stress on the ambiguity of what Johnnie was trying to do to Lina; the link charges the struggle in the car with a similar ambiguity. As the car door flies open and Lina grapples with Johnnie's hand reaching across her, (a) there is a moment when his expression really does suggest he's trying to push her

Figure 25

out (fig. 25), and (b) her terror is again eroticized: she seems in an ecstasy of fear. Then, when he does stop the car and she flees from him, he angrily grabs her by the wrists to control her, as he had on the hilltop (fig. 26). This gesture is used by Hitchcock in a number of films to express a man's aggressive attempts to dominate and control a woman: see my discussion of "Hands" in *Hitchcock's Motifs*.[27] Equally significant here, however, is the link with the hilltop scene, which Hitchcock emphasizes by suddenly introducing a spindly tree—which echoes those on the hilltop—next to the couple.

We could also compare this climactic clifftop scene with the earlier one with Beaky. Again it's as if Johnnie intended murder, but was unable to carry it through: halted, in this case, by the frenzy of Lina's panic. In addition, the scene may be paralleled with the second scene in *Rebecca* (1940). Maxim (Laurence Olivier) has returned to the clifftop where Rebecca had told him on their honeymoon of her past "depravities," and he seems about to jump off—before being stopped by an anxious call from the heroine (also played by Joan Fontaine). If Maxim *has* returned to the site of his past trauma to commit

Figure 26

suicide, the scene expresses his death drive: as he says later, when Rebecca's body is found, "I've known all along that Rebecca would win in the end." *Suspicion* is similarly suggestive. Lina is being forcibly taken back to a place equivalent to the one where she fantasized Beaky's death at Johnnie's hands, a death with which she seemed in some sense to identify. Consciously, she clearly wants to live, but it is hinted that against this are the pressures of her unconscious, seeking release from her torments in oblivion.

In the scene that follows Lina's terrified flight from the car, some sort of exculpating explanation of Johnnie's recent behavior is obviously required. But, conveniently, it's Lina who comes up with this: that Johnnie wanted to know about the untraceable poison because he was going to commit suicide. "Yes," says Johnnie, "but I saw that was a cheap way out." Since almost everything Johnnie has said about his private life has been a lie, I have no inclination whatever to believe this. Instead, I see it as Hitchcock's clue (or Johnnie's Freudian slip): it's the clifftop murder attempts on Beaky and Lina that Johnnie is really talking about. A further point here is that Johnnie says he was in Liverpool, trying to borrow money on Lina's life insurance, when Beaky died in Paris. But we have seen the envelopes of the insurance companies which wrote to Johnnie, one of them in answer to this query, and they both bear London addresses.[28] Hitchcock's main reason for showing the letters in close-up must surely be to signal that Johnnie really is lying again in this last scene.

The strained nature of the scene also registers in Lina's speech to Johnnie, which, from a feminist point of view, is pure garbage. Lina now blames herself for the state Johnnie has reached: she wasn't close enough to him; he wasn't able to confide in her. What she says is in effect a plea for women to be more "understanding" towards the problems of their men. The responsibility of the man for his furtive and criminal behavior, and for having generated such fear in his wife, is simply not mentioned. Moreover, even at this stage, when Johnnie is supposed to be reforming and finally facing up to his obligations, there's no talk of him getting a job.

The very ending of the film is problematic in a different sense. At first, Johnnie responds negatively to Lina's "Let's go home" (and face things together), but when they're in the car he does a U-turn to make the return journey. But in the shot from behind the couple that Richard Allen describes, I'm almost certain that the man making the ambiguous "snake-like coil" gesture round Lina is not Cary Grant. (The woman could be Joan Fontaine.) At this absolutely crucial point of the film, Hitchcock would seem to have used a stand-in. It's as though he had simply lost interest and couldn't be bothered to make the ending look convincing.

Suspicion begins in the dark in a railway carriage, as Johnnie enters Lina's compartment and brushes her leg. His mysteriousness—and sexuality—are thus signalled from the film's opening seconds; as the train emerges from the tunnel, he appears as the traditional tall, dark, and handsome stranger, just as she appears as the bookish, quiet, conservatively dressed spinster. The film ends with the two of them "going home" in a car, but if Lina has blossomed sexually in the interim, she has also entered into the fraught world of domestic mistrust and fear. Johnnie is still an enigma; she could indeed be going home with a man who wants to murder her. The ending of *Suspicion* really resolves very little, and conspicuously lacks the closure that the majority of Hollywood films work so hard to achieve. Marina Warner's Beast is not tamed.

In *Hitchcock's Films Revisited*, Robin Wood also reassesses *Suspicion*. Referring to the alternative ways of reading its ending, that is, from viewing Johnnie as a murderer, to viewing him as only a murderer in Lina's eyes, he writes:

> As one mentally "switches" from ending to ending, the significance of every scene changes, the apparent solidity of the narrative dissolves, the illusion of the fiction's "reality" disintegrates, the film becomes a "modernist" text in which the process of narrative is foregrounded.[29]

I don't think the film quite works like this. I think it is, rather, an "incoherent text," a term Wood uses elsewhere to characterize certain American films of the 1970s.[30] The ending is fudged but, given the competing pressures, Hitchcock had no real alternative but to fudge. That he wanted Johnnie to be a murderer becomes increasingly apparent in the later scenes, but it would have been impossible for the film to admit this unambiguously. Instead, we are left with irresolution.

My final thought about the compromise ending is speculative. I think that, just as Hitchcock wanted Johnnie to be a murderer, Alma did not. She knew that the film would be a disaster were it obvious that it was only a matter of time before Johnnie killed Lina—as in the appalling "looking back at the audience" ending Hitchcock mentioned to Bogdanovich. Patrick McGilligan reports that the ending we have was dashed out at the last minute by Hitchcock and Joan Harrison,[31] but in fact it allows just enough leeway to be read both ways: yes, Johnnie will reform and it's a happy ending; no, he won't, and it's a bleak, *noirish* ending.

Notes

Thanks to Douglas Pye and Leighton Grist for their helpful feedback on earlier versions of this essay, and to Sidney Gottlieb for his sterling editorial work.

1. Bill Krohn, "Ambivalence (*Suspicion*)," *Hitchcock Annual* 11 (2002-03): 101-03.

2. Krohn's various "research" and "revised findings," with an introduction by Ken Mogg, are gathered under the title "The Endings for *Suspicion*" at http://www.labyrinth.net.au/~muffin/suspicion.html.

3. Rick Worland, "Before and After the Fact: Writing and Reading Hitchcock's *Suspicion*,' *Cinema Journal* 41, no. 4 (summer 2002): 3-26.

4. Patrick Faubert, "The Role and Presence of Authorship in *Suspicion*," in *Hitchcock and Adaptation: On the Page and Screen*, ed. Mark Osteen (Lanham, MD: Rowman & Littlefield, 2014), 41-57.

5. Tania Modleski, "Suspicion: Collusion and Resistance in the Work of Hitchcock's Female Collaborators," in *A Companion to Alfred Hitchcock,* ed. Thomas Leitch and Leland Poague (Chichester: Wiley Blackwell, 2014), 162-80.

6. Mark Crispin Miller, "Hitchcock's Suspicions and *Suspicion*," *Modern Language Notes* 89, no. 5 (1983): 1144-86; rpt. in Miller, *Boxed-In: The Culture of TV* (Evanston: Northwestern University Press, 1988), 241-78.

7. Francis Iles, *Before the Fact* (London: Pocket Book Edition, 1952), 271.

8. Donald Spoto, *The Dark Side of Genius: The Life of Alfred Hitchcock* (London: Frederick Muller, 1983), 243.

9. François Truffaut, with Helen G. Scott, *Hitchcock* (London: Secker & Warburg, 1968), 116.

10. Ken Mogg, *The Alfred Hitchcock Story* (London: Titan Books, 1999), 79.

11. Truffaut, *Hitchcock*, 39.

12. Worland, "Before and After the Fact," 17.

13. "The Endings for *Suspicion*," post by Krohn, dated December 6, 2001.

14. "The Endings for *Suspicion*," post by Krohn, dated October 14, 2003.

15. Worland, "Before and After the Fact," 17.

16. Richard Allen, "Hitchcock or the Pleasures of Metaskepticism," in *Alfred Hitchcock: Centenary Essays,* ed. Richard Allen and S. Ishii-Gonzalès (London: BFI, 1999), 226.

17. Neil P. Hurley, *Soul in Suspense: Hitchcock's Fright and Delight* (Metuchen, NJ: Scarecrow Press, 1993), 86-87.

18. Krohn, "Ambivalence (*Suspicion*)," 110-11; Peter Bogdanovich, *Who the Devil Made It?* (New York: Ballantine Books, 1997), 509-10.

19. Pascal Kane, "*Soupçons,*" *Cahiers du Cinéma* 228 (March-April 1971), 57.

20. Marina Warner, "The Uses of Enchantment," in *Cinema and the Realms of Enchantment: Lectures, Seminars and Essays by Marina Warner and Others,* ed. Duncan Petrie (London: British Film Institute, 1993), 30.

21. For the benefit of those unfamiliar with the British educational system, and to correct Richard Allen's quite mistaken observations about Johnnie's background in "Hitchcock or the Pleasures of Metaskepticism," 227, I should point out that Johnnie and Beaky would have attended an English public school; that is, one of the boys' private schools that are fee paying and so primarily the preserve of the wealthy. These are boarding schools, patronized above all by the upper and middle classes, and whatever their merits educationally, their hierarchical regimes, at least during the period relevant to the film, encouraged humiliation and brutality. A "fagging" system—younger boys acting as "servants" to older—was not phased out until the 1970s, caning was institutionalized, vicious bullying was endemic. Thomas Hughes' novel *Tom Brown's Schooldays* (1857) offers a nineteenth-century depiction of such a school; *If. . . .* (Lindsay Anderson, 1968), albeit stylized, represents a heightening by Anderson of his own experiences at Cheltenham College. Robin Wood himself briefly attended a junior version of such a school—a "prep school"—and his account of being bullied there is recorded in *Hitchcock's Films Revisited* (New York: Columbia University Press, 1989), 372. However, one feels that Johnnie would have been popular and thrived in such an environment, and—like perhaps most of the boys who successfully navigated their way through such schools—would have emerged with a sense of entitlement. Beaky's idolization of Johnnie has all the hallmarks of a schoolboy "crush."

22. Robin Wood, *Hitchcock's Films Revisited,* 71; emphasis in the original.

23. Iles, *Before the Fact,* 219.

24. Wood, *Hitchcock's Films Revisited*, 71-72.

25. Allen, "Hitchcock or the Pleasures of Metaskepticism," 226.

26. Iles, *Before the Fact*, 92, 222.

27. Michael Walker, *Hitchcock's Motifs* (Amsterdam: Amsterdam University Press, 2005), 225-28.

28. Ken Mogg also points this out in *The Alfred Hitchcock Story*, 79.

29. Wood, *Hitchcock's Films Revisited*, 230.

30. Robin Wood, "The Incoherent Text: Narrative in the '70s," *Movie* 27/28 (winter 1980/spring 1981): 24-42; rpt. in Wood, *Hollywood from Vietnam to Reagan* (New York: Columbia University Press, 1986), 46-69.

31. Patrick McGilligan, *Alfred Hitchcock: A Life in Darkness and Light* (Chichester: John Wiley & Sons, 2003), 289.

SIDNEY GOTTLIEB

Under Capricorn *and the Hitchcockian Melodrama of Trauma, Recovery, and Remarriage*

Under Capricorn (1949), like many of Hitchcock's best films, and in fact all three of the films that he made with Ingrid Bergman, revolves around the axes of disintegration and reintegration. It is a stunning portrait of (to allude to a later film that glosses it in intriguing ways) a "woman under the influence" and her uneven and strenuous effort to navigate through and beyond extraordinary pressures: from inside, forces of circumstance, and intimate relationships. The signs of Henrietta's disintegration and distress are readily apparent, memorable, and often commented upon. Less so are the signifiers of her recovery, which occur in a roughly linear sequence.

As I move through some of the key images and scenes in the film, I'll organize and discuss these signifiers in several categories, which are discrete but also overlapping: changes in the way Henrietta looks and is looked at; her return to visibility, to herself and others; her transition from immobility to animation, passivity to action, including taking control in ways that reflect not coercive power but the restoration of executive functions and compassion; her return to speech, and especially narrativity, that is, the ability to tell and accept her story; her re-entrance into society; and the repair and transformation of her relationship with her husband, through a process that qualifies as one of remarriage as outlined in another generic context by Stanley Cavell.[1]

I have several aims in mind in focusing on all this: to be sure that these details and these plots beneath the plot, as it were, are noticed and given proper attention as we analyze the overall design and meaning of the film; to highlight the complexity, subtlety, and artistry but also the accuracy of the presentation of these elements; and also to argue for a particular understanding of what "recovery" means in the film—the achievement of real health, happiness, mutuality, and self-determination, emphatically not reintegration into or cooptation by an apparatus of conventional structures, codes of conduct, values, and "rules of the game."

Recovery from what? In a word: trauma. It is essential to recognize that, as Raymond Bellour points out, "the question of trauma and of its interpretation" is at the heart of Hitchcock's films.[2] For Hitchcock, trauma is a subject particularly suitable for cinematic representation, dramatization, and analysis, perhaps not least because he identifies it as a fundamental element of human experience, a disturbing fact of life not to be avoided and not to be forgotten. In Hitchcockian terms, trauma is both a sign and result of the eruption of the chaos world, and although his focus on trauma is sometimes taken as evidence of cruelty and misogyny, I think on the contrary that his lifelong interest in presenting images and telling stories of women (and men) under extreme duress is characterized by real sympathy, concern, and insight.

The accuracy, precision, and effectiveness of the presentation of trauma and recovery in *Under Capricorn* are remarkable. Where did this come from? It's worth briefly identifying three sources. The genius of the system is always evident in Hitchcock, and by that I mean the collaborative components of his films. The source novel is not a study of trauma in the way the film is, but sets up much of the scaffolding for and some of the critical events that figure prominently in the film. For all of Hitchcock's criticism of the screenwriters, we can safely assume that James Bridie and Hume Cronyn contributed something substantial to the shaping of this film's portrayal of trauma, a subject certainly worth further study. The contributions of the cinematographer, Jack Cardiff, in visualizing Henrietta's state of mind, the details of the traumatic conditions that continue around her, and the stages of her recovery certainly need to be acknowledged and analyzed, as Ed Gallafent does so expertly in his essay on the film.[3] And Ingrid Bergman's acting is surely one of the most important reasons why *Under Capricorn* is not "only a movie," as Hitchcock often archly claimed, but "more than a movie": one that conveys a vivid impression of a woman succumbing to, resisting, and then finally overcoming numerous soul-crushing experiences, conditions, and impulses.

Then there is the genius of the genre: perhaps most prominently, melodrama—one of the home genres of trauma (so much so that it in fact often makes sense to speak of "melotrauma")—is a guiding and shaping force for Hitchcock's understanding and representation of Henrietta's past and present circumstances, state of mind, options, and actions.[4] Hitchcock not only relies on but in key ways adapts and transforms melodrama, perhaps in part under the influence of other generic models, like the romance, especially the fairy tale and Shakespearean rather than chivalric romance, and, perhaps most surprisingly, comedy, broadly defined. Hitchcock always operates across several genres, and *Under Capricorn* shows how, to use Cavell's terms, the melodrama of the unknown woman—a woman's unknownness to herself and to others—can be overcome by the restorative power and strategies that characterize the comedy of remarriage: these include acknowledgment, conversation, benign exercises of power, interactive play and play-acting, engagement, intelligence, and trust.[5]

And finally, easily overlooked in this age of sometimes excessive anti-auteurism, let's not underestimate the genius of the genius: we should credit Hitchcock properly for his sensitivity, empathy, intuitive understanding, artistic ingenuity, and lifelong determination in artistically grappling with and representing trauma. And while this is meant as deserved personal praise, it is also meant as a way of reinforcing the value of studying Hitchcock's films intertextually, attentive to how his films interconnect and often usefully gloss one another. In trying to understand Henrietta in *Under Capricorn* it is extremely valuable to place her alongside Alice in *Blackmail* (1929) and Marnie in a triptych that might well be named *Three Sisters*.

There is no doubt from the very beginning of the film that Henrietta is a traumatized woman, in fact a multiply traumatized woman, someone who, as one clinician defines post-traumatic stress disorder, has been

> exposed to a horrendous event "that involved actual or threatened death or serious injury, or a threat to the physical integrity of self or others," causing "intense fear, helplessness, or horror," which results in a variety of manifestations: intrusive reexperiencing of the event ... persistent and crippling avoidance ... and increased arousal (insomnia, hypervigilance, or irritability).[6]

The original trauma is from something she did rather than something that was done to her or witnessed others doing: she shot and killed her brother, who was attempting to stop her runaway marriage and was threatening her and Sam (Joseph Cotten) with a gun. Hitchcock recognizes that the fact that this action may be legally and morally justifiable does not necessarily lessen its harrowing consequences in, to use Elaine Scarry's relevant terms, "unmaking" Henrietta's mind and world.[7] You do not have to be a "guilty" murderer or accomplice like Macbeth and Lady Macbeth to suffer the psychological devastation from killing someone, one sign of which is the overall feeling that, in Shakespeare's words, "Confusion now hath made his masterpiece" (*Macbeth* 2.3.66). We remember the shrunken head in *Under Capricorn* primarily as it is weaponized by Milly (Margaret Leighton), used in effect to force flashbacks upon Henrietta that will torture and perhaps kill her. But more broadly it is a Shakespearean touch, an objective correlative of her primal trauma, a powerful signifier reinforcing the horrifying message that David J. Morris describes very precisely as at the core of post-traumatic life: that "Trauma is the savagery of the universe made manifest within us," a savagery of violence and meaninglessness.[8]

I am not trying to turn trauma into an abstraction, but rather to acknowledge that it is a metaphysical and epistemological as well as physical and emotional wound. And again, Henrietta's trauma is compound: in addition to her distress over killing someone, she is overwhelmed by the pressures of secrecy and feelings of irresponsibility and empathic pain (I prefer those terms rather than "guilt" or "shame") over the fact that her husband has suffered for taking the blame for her act; years of alienation, "hot misery," insecurity, and other horrors while Sam was in prison that are not specified but are tangible and ravaging; and then new rounds of social prejudice and also humiliation and physical abuse at the hands of Milly. All this leaves her dissociated, distracted, disconnected, lost. She is the archetypal refugee, and the words from Tom Petty's classic and penetrating rock song ring true: she is left to "revel in her abandon."[9]

All this is what Henrietta emerges from, and in what follows I briefly highlight key details that chart this recovery. In the memorable words of one of the most insightful commentators on trauma, Bessel van der Kolk, the "body keeps the score," and tells the story—and much of Henrietta's story is told by her body, her face and eyes in particular, and revolves around what we might call visuality, which includes several components. We can accurately gauge Henrietta's state of mind by watching the fluctuations and directions of her gaze. I include a gallery of gazes (figs. 1-9), each of which would be worth analyzing in detail in its specific context and as part of an unfolding pattern in the film, to illustrate some of the many moments when her disturbed mood is shown by an averted gaze (figs. 4, 5, and 9), an upward (figs. 3 and 7) or especially a downward gaze (figs. 2, 6, and 8), or an unfocused look into the distance (fig. 1), all contributing to our awareness that she is, to use Charles Barr's term, a "tranced" woman, a recurrent figure in Hitchcock's films.[10] Gallafent discusses these looks insightfully as a foundational element in the structure of *Under Capricorn*, and his essay supports an even broader claim: that we should never watch any Hitchcock film without recognizing this iconography of looks as one of Hitchcock's characteristic and fundamental expressive techniques.[11]

Figure 1

Figure 2

Figure 3

Figure 4

Figure 5

Figure 6

Figure 7

Figure 8

Figure 9

But throughout the film there are also looks counterpointed to those shown in the first gallery of illustrations, and even though I don't have the time here to trace the complex choreography of how they alternate and interact with those looks, the second gallery (figs. 10-14) at least shows a sample of moments when Henrietta looks directly into someone's eyes, evoking new-found courage, confidence, and a leap into mutuality.

Figure 10

Figure 11

Figure 12

Figure 13

Figure 14

Robin Wood talks movingly about how Ingrid Bergman's films often revolve around somehow getting her to regain her smile.[12] *Under Capricorn* is a good example of how a Bergman film also revolves around getting her to regain the ability to look someone directly in the eyes — an accomplishment that we as spectators intuitively recognize and appreciate and that clinical researchers have confirmed has a neurological effect, and is a victory over the disruption of prefrontal cortex functioning that is a result of trauma.[13] And, as we see several times in *Under Capricorn*, it is truly a magical moment when Henrietta looks at someone in the eyes and smiles (see, for example, figs. 10, 11, and 14). Furthermore, as she gains strength and confidence, even gazes and expressions that might earlier be taken as indications of distress can be taken as more positive signs: at key moments as the film progresses, Henrietta's look into the distance is not the "thousand-yard stare" at nothingness that afflicts her, as seen for example in figure 1, but a more hopeful acknowledgment of a supportive and encouraging past or future (fig. 15) or a new sense of determination (fig. 16); and even a look downward, which is the universal gesture of diffidence, shame, isolation, and dependence, is transformed into a sign of gratefulness and connection — as when near the end of the film she acknowledges the actions of Adare (Michael Wilding) to help save Sam (fig. 17).

Henrietta is caught not only in a crisis of visuality but also in a crisis of visibility. A major part of the latter involves her unwillingness and inability to look at herself. Trauma involves the dissolution and disappearance of the self.[14] Adare helps Henrietta overcome this, in ways that may seem trivial and even suspicious or problematic, but turn out to be beneficent. The two mirror sequences in the film are brief but pivotal, not only because of their effect on Henrietta, but also because of what they establish about Adare's character and role in the film. The film flirts with presenting Adare as the lover in a love triangle. But he is more interesting and prominent as part of a therapeutic triangle: as an artist helping remake Henrietta — and far from being a rough draft

Figure 15

Figure 16

Figure 17

of Scottie Ferguson, he is a Pygmalion gone right, not wrong—and even as a kind of wizard. In Proppian terms, he is a helper or donor, someone with good intentions and a magical object.

Adare has a spontaneous and bright idea: in order for Henrietta to be herself, she needs to see herself. He first turns a window into a mirror (fig. 18), which shows her as she is at the moment, and then soon after gives her a mirror, unwrapping it to create a moment of revelation of who she has in the interim become (fig. 19)—remade at least insofar as her appearance has changed markedly, readying her for respect and resocialization.

Figure 18

Figure 19

The quizzical expression on her face and the details of her outfit—there is a stark contrast between her introduction as "undressed" and her sudden emergence as fashionably over-dressed—perhaps indicate that she is not yet entirely comfortable with the process of finding and constructing and adjusting to her self. But the mirror sequences are critical moments of recognition, essential to her further development.

I want to continue to address the theme of her return to visibility, but with what may seem to be a slight digression to address several critical events that happen next in the film under the related category of the reanimation of Henrietta. The film shows a shift in Henrietta from passivity and either immobility or restricted or wayward and wandering movement to activity and freer and more directed and purposeful motion. (One of the challenges throughout the film is Henrietta's quest to gain the mobility of the camera—with the qualification that some kinds of mobility are better than others.) The second kitchen sequence captures Henrietta's reanimation visually and powerfully conveys its significance as a part of her recovery. Using the rubrics that describe components of trauma and recovery may deepen our sense of what is really happening here: this scene is not as much about the clash between Henrietta and Milly for dominance in the household as it is an illustration of the restoration of Henrietta's executive functions—exactly those functions typically disabled by trauma.

This sequence also displays other motives and strategies that writers on trauma specify as critical in recovery. "Work, work, work" is one of the mantras of emerging from trauma, and it is enacted here by Henrietta. Asserting one's control is often designated in general as a key element of growth and recovery, but more particularly writers on trauma emphasize that the "benign use of power" is the "foundation of the self" post-trauma, and the kitchen sequence dramatizes a shift from abusive to benign power, orchestrated by Henrietta. And for all that this sequence seems to be about power, it is ultimately about charity and connection. Among many other commentators, Laurence Gonzales, in his important book on

Figure 20

Surviving Survival, says that "helping others is one of the most therapeutic steps you can take . . . . Helping someone else is as important as getting help."[15] What is most striking and should be most memorable about this sequence is not the assertion of her (temporary) victory over Milly and the gaining of the keys, but Henrietta's kindness, her linking with, not lording over, the servant women (fig. 20), conveyed by a tableau of mutual, respectful, and supportive gazes shared with others who are clearly also victims of abuse, and her restoration of beneficent order—all this preceded by her burning of the whip of trauma.

The Governor's Ball illustrates several of the components and movements that I have been tracking. It is of course a kind of watershed moment of her movement away from loneliness and disconnection and toward re-entrance into society, complete with the continuing makeover of her appearance, as well as a further reinforcement of her self-confidence and poise visible in her body language (the film oscillates between her being prone and upright), captured memorably even before she arrives at the ball by her grand descent on the staircase (fig. 21). And the ball sequence furthers her reanimation, not only in showing her mobility in leaving the house and walking in a very self-possessed manner at the ball but also by dancing: specifically dancing a

Figure 21

Figure 22

waltz, which is charged with particular meaning as a signifier of something new (a perfect dance for the new Henrietta); unconventional and daring, characterized by free rather than constrained and formal, prearranged movement; and also enacted by couples rather than groups—a slight but perhaps not insignificant part of a cluster of reminders, including the film's final image, that the formation of the couple is a central concern.

But I want to focus briefly how this sequence adds new dimensions to the themes of visuality and visibility. Her self-assurance is evident not only in her body language but in the

Figure 23

way she looks directly ahead as she walks, and looks directly into the eyes of the Governor as they talk (fig. 22). Now for a point that may be a bit more problematic. She is presented as a central part of the spectacle of the ball: in the way that the camera shoots and frames her, and also in the repeated views of her being looked at by people at the ball. These details, as well as others in the film, support what may initially sound like a heretical claim: to-be-looked-atness, to use Laura Mulvey's unforgettable term, can be a good thing, and in the context of Henrietta's recovery from trauma it is at least sometimes emphatically therapeutic.[16] Much depends, of course, on the way one is looked at, and there is not much good to be said about, to adopt Prufrock's words, being "fixed in a formulating gaze," especially one of manipulation and control—like Milly's gaze at Henrietta (fig. 23). But clinicians agree that one of the "critical issues" in trauma recovery "is being truly heard and seen by the people around us, feeling that we are held in someone's mind and heart."[17] Interpersonal intimacy, as I'll discuss in a moment, is of course essential, and this is often conveyed by one person looking directly at another, and two people looking directly at each other. So is what we might call "public intimacy," established by looks of acknowledgment, respect, and connection in a group setting, as seen in figure 22.

The ball ends in a real setback, a moment of disruption and humiliation that is deeply upsetting to Henrietta. But this is immediately followed by a step forward, in the confession sequence—one that in fact initiates a series of confessions and confessions about confessing—which is among other things a stunning illustration of the importance of regaining narrativity and one's voice. Numerous kinds of reconnection are shown in the film. Up to this point the emphasis has been on reconnection in space, by movement and physical activity and contacts with others. Now there is a turn to reconnection in time, specifically by recognizing and reintegrating the past, which is accomplished by Henrietta telling her story, simultaneously to herself and someone else. Reconstructing in a coherent form the history of the trauma is, according to most clinicians, a necessary (although not in itself sufficient) part of reconstructing the traumatized self, and Judith Herman speaks for many in noting that "sharing the traumatic experience with others is a precondition for the restitution of a sense of a meaningful world."[18]

Hitchcock prepares for this sequence carefully, while still setting it up so that Henrietta's revelation comes as a surprise. Earlier in the film, Sam tells Adare that "If you can get her talking about old times, that might help," and though what he has in mind are the happy days of Henrietta's youth, his advice about the efficacy of a "talking cure" is as well-founded as it is ironic. There are early moments that show Henrietta gradually moving toward regaining her voice and telling her story: for example, in the brief scene where she dictates part of a letter to Adare's sister. But her long monologue after the ball is a breakthrough, and one of the dramatic highlights of the film. Rohmer and Chabrol insightfully point out that "The fact that the heroine finally speaks is as important as what she tells."[19] Regaining her voice, moving "from silence to speech," is a critical marker of Henrietta's development and recovery. But for all that Rohmer and Chabrol stress the centrality of confession throughout Hitchcock's films as a legacy of his Catholicism, *Under Capricorn* confirms that confessional narrativity can be powerfully therapeutic even apart from any religious context. As both Gallafent and Richard Allen show, there are indeed religious references in the film, but healing in *Under Capricorn* happens without churches and priests—and, I might add, without clinicians of any kind.[20]

The reestablishment of intimacy is often described as the final stage of recovery from trauma, and in *Under Capricorn* it is both an end and a means—something we seek and something we need in order to get what we seek. There are different forms of intimacy in the film: Sam and Adare are intimate, perhaps surprisingly so, almost from the very beginning; and the intimacy—physical at times—between Henrietta and Adare is critically important, but is one of love without being set in a relationship of lovers, a distinction with a real difference. Henrietta and Sam are the lovers in the film, and while the film is fundamentally about the restoration of Henrietta's self, it is also about the restoration of her marriage with Sam. Their love and marriage are, to say the least, sorely tested. They are a traumatized couple—not only insofar as interpersonal relationships are inevitably casualties of trauma but also because each one of them is traumatized. Two scenes in particular dramatize the complex and painful process of their recovery and remarriage.

First, the climactic scene in the bedroom with Milly. Unlike the parallel sequence at the end of *Notorious* (1946), this one does not reduce to a completely helpless and vulnerable woman saved by a man who somewhat magically and suddenly is moved to a moment of clarity and conventionally heroic action. Instead, we see Henrietta's remarkable determination and energy, and her partnership with Sam in her rescue and their rescue. Rohmer and Chabrol describe the shot of Henrietta's face during the preparation of Milly's assault on her as "one of the most significant close-ups in the entire history of cinema," packed with a Dostoyevskian richness of meaning.[21] Her tears are visible, but to me this is not primarily a scene of weeping, penitential or otherwise. The shot—actually a series of repeated shots—shows Henrietta's pain but also her increasingly clear, knowing, focused, resistant, empowered and empowering gaze and

Figure 24

new strength (fig. 24). Her subsequent cry of help to Sam is not one of pathetic inadequacy but a call for him to join in a shared struggle, and when Sam enters, they overcome their moments of doubt and pain through remarkably courageous, honest, and intelligent declarations and conversation, and are able to recognize the truth, dispel the immediate threat, and reconfirm their love, intimacy, and marriage.

What follows soon after is for me one of the most memorable moments in the film, and what I think of as one of its multiple endings (a structural feature of many of Hitchcock's films). Henrietta comes down the staircase again, but not like before in a display of costume and assured beauty, and certainly not like Alicia at a comparable moment in *Notorious*, unable to even walk to safety without Devlin's aid. She walks down to meet and rejoin Sam, and together they re-define, re-declare, and re-consecrate their relationship. All this is brilliantly conveyed by the entire sequence, but one image can stand as a stunning synecdoche. Here we see the past, immediate, and inevitably ongoing strain transcended without vanishing. They do not look directly at each other, but these are no averted gazes: their effort is to rejoin. Their faces are turned downward, but not in abjection. Athough their eyes are closed, their expressions and body language convey intense emotion and deep vision, and although the frame composition

Figure 25

Figure 26

is disharmonious, this is a moment of breakthrough and reconnection (fig. 25). Hitchcock's wisdom—here and in other films as well—is like that of the Japanese art of *kintsugi*, whereby precious and fragile artifacts are restored, but rather than being erased, the cracks are highly visible, part of the repaired beauty and strength. The fact that trauma is indelible does not undermine the possibility, the reality of recovery.

If *Vertigo* (1958) is arguably the highpoint of Hitchcock's romantic irony, agony, and ecstasy, *Under Capricorn* is arguably his peak illustration of a romanticism that ends up beyond the unpleasure principle. For me, the image of Sam and Henrietta on the staircase (fig. 25) coexists with, lies beneath, makes possible the concluding image of the film (fig. 26), showing the couple alone in the distance (Adare and the crowd have just pulled away from them), just after waving, a gesture of both goodbye and hello. While this is by no means a "happy ever after" ending, it is a subdued enunciation of the thrilling and satisfying experience of survival captured wonderfully in the title of an early volume of poems by D.H. Lawrence: *Look! We Have Come Through!*

We desperately need this message. Again, Tom Petty's haunting and insistent words are relevant and moving: "You don't have to live like a refugee." Life is love, loss, and — maybe — recovery. Everything else is conversation. This is the stunning dramatization, lesson, and hope at the heart of *Under Capricorn*.

Notes

Early encouragement from Stéphane Duckett, from his perspective as a deeply knowledgeable Hitchcockian and an experienced clinician, was enormously helpful in overcoming my initial — and ongoing — nervousness in pursuing a topic that is so complex and challenging, to say the least. Conversations with Rick Grigg and Diana Mille, especially after we watched the film together, allowed me to learn much from their remarkable personal and professional insight into the dynamics and representations of trauma. Sonia Erlich, who shares something important with me every time I see her, steered me to the eye-opening and life-changing work of Bessel van der Kolk, which then led me to many other writings that have helped me to at least start to traverse the continent of trauma. I tried out various ideas about *Under Capricorn* in exchanges with Richard Allen, John Bruns, and Tom Leitch, and benefited greatly from their responses. The opportunity to present this paper at the *Under Capricorn at 70* conference, organized by Stéphane Duckett and Charles Barr at King's College, London (September 5-6, 2019), gave me valuable feedback that I have tried to incorporate in this slightly revised version. And as I was preparing the essay for publication, Renata Jackson's detailed and thoughtful comments saved me from numerous errors and infelicities.

I consulted ebook versions of several of the works below. Since their pagination depends on the format of the software used to read them and is therefore inconsistent, when I cite them I refer to the chapter in which the quoted material appears.

1. Stanley Cavell, *Pursuits of Happiness: The Hollywood Comedy of Remarriage* (Cambridge, Mass: Harvard University Press, 1984).

2. Raymond Bellour, "The *Marnie* Color," in Catherine Liu, John Mowitt, Thomas Pepper, and Jakki Spicer, eds., *The Dreams of Interpretation: A Century Down the Royal Road* (Minneapolis: University of Minnesota Press, 2007), 253-62, at 254.

3. Ed Gallafent, "The Dandy and the Magdalen: Interpreting the Long Take in Hitchcock's *Under Capricorn*," in John Gibbs and Douglas Pye, eds., *Style and Meaning: Studies in the Detailed Analysis of Film* (New York: Manchester University Press, 2005), 68-84.

4. See Robin Wood, "Star and Auteur: Hitchcock's Films with Bergman," in *Hitchcock's Films Revisited*, rev. ed. (New York: Columbia University Press, 2002), 303-35, esp 327-28.

5. Stanley Cavell, *Contesting Tears: The Hollywood Melodrama of the Unknown Woman* (Chicago: University of Chicago Press, 1996).

6. Bessel van der Kolk, *The Body Keeps the Score: Brain, Mind, and Body in the Healing of Trauma* (New York: Penguin Books, 2014), ebook, chapter 10, quoting the American Psychiatric Association's *Diagnostic and Statistical Manual of Mental Disorders*.

7. Elaine Scarry, *The Body in Pain: The Making and Unmaking of the World* (New York: Oxford University Press, 1985).

8. David J. Morris, *The Evil Hours: A Biography of Post-Traumatic Stress Disorder* (Boston: Houghton Mifflin Harcourt, 2015), ebook, chapter 2.

9. Tom Petty and Mike Campbell, "Refugee," on *Damn the Torpedoes*. Backstreet Records, 1980, album.

10. Charles Barr, *English Hitchcock* (Moffat: Cameron & Hollis, 1999), 173.

11. Gallafent, "The Dandy and the Magdalen," 70-75. I discuss in detail the expressive function of numerous ways of looking and "acting with the eyes" in Hitchcock's films in "The Variety of Gazes in *Vertigo*," in *Haunted by* Vertigo: *Hitchcock's Masterpiece Then and Now*, ed. Sidney Gottlieb and Donal Martin (London: John Libbey/Indiana University Press, 2021).

12. Wood, "Star and Auteur: Hitchcock's Films with Bergman," 317-18.

13. Van der Kolk, *The Body Keeps the Score*, chapter 6.

14. Van der Kolk, *The Body Keeps the Score*, chapter 3.

15. Laurence Gonzales, *Surviving Survival: The Art and Science of Resilience* (New York: Norton, 2013), ebook, chapters 1 and 13.

16. See Laura Mulvey, "Visual Pleasure and Narrative Cinema," *Screen* 16, no. 3 (1975): 6-18.

17. Van der Kolk, *The Body Keeps the Score*, chapter 5; see also chapter 4.

18. Judith L. Herman, *Trauma and Recovery: The Aftermath of Violence—From Domestic Abuse to Political Terror* (1992; rpt. New York: Basic Books, 2015), ebook, chapter 3.

19. Eric Rohmer and Claude Chabrol, *Hitchcock: The First Forty-Four Films*, trans. Stanley Hochman (New York: Frederick Ungar Publishing Co., 1979), 103.

20. Gallafent, "The Dandy and the Magdalen"; Richard Allen, "*Under Capricorn*: Hitchcock, Melodrama, and the Christian Imagination," *Hitchcock Annual* 23 (2019): 107-40. In the studies about trauma that I have read, religion is conspicuously absent as a factor in the understanding of and recovery from trauma. Van der Kolk in particular is adamant about the non-clinical and non-institutional avenues of healing.

21. Rohmer and Chabrol, *Hitchcock: The First Forty-Four Films*, 99.

Thomas Leitch

Queering the Cattle:
Hitchcock and Performance

Dan Callahan, *The Camera Lies: Acting for Hitchcock.* New York: Oxford University Press, 2020. xviii + 251 pp. $34.95 cloth.

Considering the critical attention that has been lavished on so many aspects of Alfred Hitchcock's films, the relative neglect of his collaborations with performers is as striking in its way as Hitchcock's own well-documented neglect of performers who cried out in vain for more active direction. Doris Day despaired over her leading performance in the American remake of *The Man Who Knew Too Much* because Hitchcock "never said anything to me, before or during or after a scene, and I was crushed"; Thelma Ritter emerged from *Rear Window* with the wisdom that "if Hitchcock liked what you did, he said nothing. If he didn't, he looked like he was going to throw up."[1] Apart from the anecdotes liberally sprinkled through Hitchcock's biographies about the director's relationships with the actors who brought his nightmares to life, critical studies of acting in Hitchcock include James Naremore's penetrating chapters on Cary Grant's performance in *North by Northwest* and on *Rear Window* as a performance text; Doug Tomlinson's "'They Should Be Treated Like Cattle': Hitchcock and the Question of Performance"; Susan White's essay "A Surface Collaboration: Hitchcock and Performance"; Carey Martin's "The Master of Suspense and the Acrobat of the Drawing Room: How the Relationship of Cary Grant and Alfred Hitchcock Shaped Their Collaboration in *Suspicion, Notorious, To Catch a Thief,* and *North by Northwest*"; and Lesley L.

Coffin's *Hitchcock's Stars: Hitchcock and the Hollywood Studio System*.[2] None of these contributions, not even the last, amounts to a compelling full-dress examination of acting in Hitchcock's films.

Now at long last Dan Callahan has undertaken to provide just such a study. He approaches his subject not as a Hitchcockian—his brief bibliography does not include any of these earlier books or essays, and he nods only rarely and briefly at previous Hitchcock scholarship—but as a highly regarded expert on Hollywood acting, the author of *Barbara Stanwyck: The Miracle Woman* (2012), *Vanessa: The Life of Vanessa Redgrave* (2014), *The Art of American Screen Acting, 1912-1960* (2018), and *The Art of American Screen Acting, 1960 to Today* (2019). The warm reception that has greeted all of these projects, especially the last two, would seem to make Callahan the logical candidate to write a definitive study of acting in Hitchcock's films.

Callahan enters a field in which he has only a few competitors with several notable advantages over them. His volume is extensive in its coverage, discussing every one of Hitchcock's completed features from *The Pleasure Garden* to *Family Plot*. He displays an engaging zest for his subject, and his confident, intimate prose makes that zest infectious. Most important, he assumes from the start that acting for Hitchcock is an obvious subject for a monograph in a way that acting for George Cukor or Martin Scorsese or Quentin Tarantino would not be. This is partly because of the contempt for performers Hitchcock communicated in his famous pronouncement, "Actors are cattle," which was scarcely mitigated by his elaboration years later: "I would never say such an unfeeling, rude thing about actors at all. . . . what I probably said was that all actors should be *treated* like cattle" (quoted in Callahan ix). Instead of concurring or registering ritual disapproval of the director's famous remark, Callahan shrewdly contextualizes it:

> He made his "actors are cattle" statement because the [stage-trained] English actors he was working with in

the 1930s, like John Gielgud, who starred in *Secret Agent* (1936), and Michael Redgrave, who was the lead in *The Lady Vanishes* (1938), treated movie work too lightly. . . . Gielgud didn't take Hitchcock's movie thrillers as seriously as he did his Shakespeare, and this hurt and annoyed Hitchcock. (xiv)

Callahan is equally deft in distinguishing between what might be called actors' cinema, which seeks to evoke emotions by presenting them explicitly, especially in the "'big scenes for players" that were "anathema" to "Hitchcock's approach" (94), and directors' cinema, which seeks to evoke emotions by presenting familiar-seeming characters in extraordinary situations created as powerfully by writing, lighting, cutting, and scoring as by performing. Hitchcock, according to Callahan, "favored major stars for his chase films because they were more likely to make the audience worry about the characters, because a star, Hitchcock said, is like one of the family. He wanted his audience to act and supply emotion to the large heads of the stars on the large screen, and so he didn't want the actors to do too much emoting" (xiv).

The greatest value of Callahan's framing premise is the number of strong arguments it generates. Even when these arguments are familiar, Callahan finds novel ways to present them. "Hitchcock continually said in interviews that his ideal actor was someone who could do nothing well" (xv), he reports: someone like Louise Brooks or Gerald Du Maurier or Leo G. Carroll or, yes, Tippi Hedren. But Callahan goes on to describe the negative acting Hitchcock sought in more specific terms: "He saw that an actor could register an emotion better if they were already caught up in one emotion, or in the midst of some action, and then caught up quickly in another emotion" (xv). Because "what Hitchcock really liked were faces in some kind of transition" (xii), he "wanted the face of the actor to be ambiguous enough sometimes so that the audience could read thoughts or emotions into the face. Hitchcock is always asking us to wonder what might be the real emotion on a face and what has to be supplied by the person watching that face" (xiv). Hence "the sense of versatility in a stage actor, of convincingly being or portraying something you are not, was anathema to Hitchcock, and to many of the best film directors from Jean Renoir to Howard Hawks" (xv), because he conceives of performance not as an impersonation but as a collaboration between performers, directors, and audiences. Having compared Hitchcock to Renoir and Hawks, Callahan pushes further in an utterly unexpected direction: "What Hitchcock wanted from his actors is finally not too far from what Robert Bresson wanted from his own mainly non-professional actor-models: the mysterious and engaging workings of what can always be called soul" (xvi). Whether or not readers are convinced by the analogy between Hitchcock and Bresson or the reference to soul as a foundational term of acting, they are likely to be provoked to new reflections on the relations between stars and non-professional actor-models and between actors, directors, audiences, and the performances they collaborate in creating. The power to invite such reflections makes Callahan's ten-page introduction perhaps the best general introduction to Hitchcockian performance to date.

Callahan finds the negative acting Hitchcock valued so highly in some unexpected places. Although he has little patience for Ivor Novello's "drama queen posturing" in *The Lodger,* he notes that as long as "he 'does nothing' in close-up and keeps his face opaque, Novello is a pleasingly ambiguous figure who invites curiosity and attention" (15). In sum, "he is at his best in *The Lodger* when he silently broods and trusts to presence and at his worst when most active, when he is 'doing' something or trying to convey unrest" or "cringing and shuddering" in a way that involves "seeming gay to the camera" (15). Callahan is even more critical of Benita Hume's one-shot performance in *Easy Virtue* as the switchboard operator who overhears John Whittaker's marriage proposal to Larita Filton, a performance Hitchcock singled out for special praise. Even though "her facial expressions do get the meaning of the scene very clearly across," they do so because "Hume forces the expressions on her face in a staccato, obvious way, as if each turn in the conversation is an electric shock that jolts her" (24). Unlike Edna Best and Leslie Banks, who "do nothing, yes, but they don't do nothing well" as the parents whose daughter has been kidnapped in *The Man Who Knew Too Much* (1934), Joan Barry and Percy Marmont, in the shipboard scene in *Rich and Strange* that brings them so close to romance before they back away, provide "some of the best acting, or pure *being* and interacting, in all of Hitchcock's work" (47). For Callahan, Hitchcock's cinema is an actor's cinema, "but only for a certain type of actor" (95): not Method actors like Montgomery Clift or Paul Newman, not "dominant stars like [Charles] Laughton" (93); not Barbara Stanwyck, who "lets an audience in on all kinds of subtle gradations in her own thoughts and feelings," for "in a Hitchcock movie this would be like showing how the magic trick is done" (94). Discussing the impossibility of Hitchcock's directing Stanwyck or Katharine Hepburn or Bette Davis or Greta Garbo, Callahan spins off one of his happiest generalizations:

> The more extravagantly particular and expressive an actor, the less they were useful for Hitchcock. His films needed people in them who could look one way and turn out to be another, and so the performances in his movies are always best and most resonant when he can cast an undervalued player against type, or a theater actor who is used to turning on a dime. The biggest and most distinctive and managing stars cannot give Hitchcock what he needs. (94)

Instead of showcasing master technicians of screen acting, the director drew some of his best performances from stars like Herbert Marshall in *Murder!*, "an ideal Hitchcock actor: a little phlegmatic, maybe, but able to suggest that there are fires banked down in him" (37), and Joseph Cotten, who "has a neither-here-nor-there sort of waiting quality that made him an ideal Hitchcock actor" (123) in *Shadow of a Doubt*, and Tallulah Bankhead, whose "bad-girl manner and very fast, surprising comic timing is vital to *Lifeboat*" (128). Because "he wants the audience to emote, not the actors" (xi), he approaches the television series *Alfred Hitchcock Presents* not by emphasizing "the impersonality of 21st-century evil where men try to kill as many people as possible" (188), but, as Hitchcock put it, by bringing "murder back into the home, where it belongs" (*National Observer*, 15 August 1966). He is especially drawn to "murder plots [that] revolve around the difficulty or impossibility of getting a divorce" in the 1950s: "The trick is getting our attention with a setup and then goading our uncertainty until we can emote for him in front of the TV set just as we did for the larger movie screen" (188). It may seem illogical to say that "Hitchcock wants us to do the acting most of the time" (188), but it is very much in keeping with the emotional audience response Hitchcock envisioned when he predicted a future in which "we won't even have to make a movie—there'll be electrodes implanted in their brains, and we'll just press different buttons and they'll go 'ooooh' and 'aaaah' and we'll frighten them, and make them laugh. Won't that be wonderful?"[3] Hitchcock follows Aristotle in emphasizing plot over character, and when his audience emotes, they are typically either imputing emotions to ambiguous characters or reacting vicariously to the fraught situations in which those characters find themselves, as Hitchcock exulted to see Joseph Cotten's wife react involuntarily during a screening of *Rear Window* to the moment when Lisa Fremont is threatened with capture by Lars Thorwald by "turn[ing] to her husband and whisper[ing], 'Do something, do something!'"[4]

For all its strengths, the force of *The Camera Lies* is compromised by several weaknesses. The most obvious of these are structural. In his determination to provide coverage of all of Hitchcock's completed features, Callahan plows dutifully through the director's corpus, film by film, often scene by scene, allowing the sequence of scenes and films to structure his argument. The resulting cavalcade sometimes swamps the argument under the chronological sequence of events in a given film or the films in a given decade, and occasionally raises the suspicion that Callahan has lost sight of his own argument and is simply describing the passing parade. The comprehensiveness implied by his film-by-film approach is undermined by his inevitably uneven coverage of different films, as when his eight-page chapter on *The Ring, Downhill, The Farmer's Wife, Easy Virtue, Champagne,* and *The Manxman* is followed by an eight-page chapter devoted entirely to *Blackmail. Blackmail* certainly occupies a more pivotal role in Hitchcock's career than any of the six silent films that immediately precede it, but Callahan never makes a case for its greater interest as a performance text. In fact, he is largely critical of the central performance in the film's synch-sound version: "neither the look of [Anny] Ondra nor the sound of [Joan] Barry is suitable for Alice White," since "Ondra looks as if she would have no problem sleeping with Crewe (Cyril Ritchard), a lecherous artist, whereas judging by the sound of Barry's genteel voice, Alice never would have gone up to 'see his etchings' to begin with" (28).

The suspicion that Callahan chooses some films to linger over longer than others not necessarily because their performances are richer but simply because he likes them better is deepened by the language in which he dismisses the ones that do not make the grade. Of the three paragraphs he devotes to *The Trouble with Harry* (whose ritualistically decorous performance style, best expressed by the question Miss Graveley asks Captain Wiles when she sees him dragging a dead body by its feet through the woods—"What seems to be the trouble, Captain?"—certainly stands out from that of most Hitchcock's films), only the second deals with the film's acting:

> Shirley MacLaine made her film debut here as a young widow with a small boy, and she seems uncomfortable with all the wordy dialogue provided by John Michael Hayes. She doesn't really know what she's doing, but she pretends that she does while a miscast John Forsythe tries to play a randy Abstract Expressionist painter. (183–84)

Of the film as a whole, Callahan merely observes that "there isn't a whole lot going on in it" (183).

Offhandedly dismissive remarks like these suggest that Callahan is winking at audience members who are already so familiar with *The Trouble with Harry* that they do not need more than a hint to move them to nod in agreement. But this assumption is very much at odds with his scene-by-scene summaries of films from *The Pleasure Garden* to *The Wrong Man*, which tend to assume that his audience has never seen these films. On balance, Callahan does not seem to have decided once and for all what his audience already knows and doesn't know, or who his audience is. The best guess, that he is writing for acting buffs who may never have thought about, or even seen, Hitchcock's films, is supported by his inveterate habit of interrupting his analyses of particular performances for a good anecdote, however tangential it might be to the point at hand. The most striking of these tangents are frankly speculative. Describing the scene in *The Lodger* in which Daisy has locked the bathroom door so that she can take a bath, he notes:

> And this brings up a key Hitchcockian question. Could Janet Leigh's Marion Crane have locked the bathroom door when she takes a shower in *Psycho*? Norman-in-drag-as-Mrs. Bates gets into Marion's room with his key, but is there a lock on the bathroom door Marion could have secured? Imagine "Norma" Bates's frustration, standing there with a butcher knife and unable to get in! Of course, stabbing Marion to death in her robe as she enters the bedroom after her shower just wouldn't have the same zing to it for either Mrs. Bates or the audience. (16)

Later, reflecting on Iris Henderson's dismay in *The Lady Vanishes* when no one believes her insistence that the substitute Miss Froy who confronts her aboard the train bears no resemblance to the elderly woman she chatted with earlier, Callahan poses a series of questions that rapidly spiral away from the moment and the film:

Can she be sure? Can we be sure? Was Miss Froy only a movie? We can watch Hitchcock movies over and over again all our lives and still not be sure about what's coming next or what just happened. His movies, like life itself, are finally a sleight of hand. Can you be *sure* of what you saw? What if, say, Madeleine Carroll suddenly entered midway into *The Lady Vanishes* with her hair dyed black instead of its usual frothy blonde meringue, and she was as sure of herself and self-loving as Lockwood's Iris, and she told Redgrave's Gilbert that *she* was Iris? Can we really be so sure she wasn't or isn't? Maybe Hitchcock could decide to rip Lockwood up like a Walt Disney drawing and insert Carroll instead. Taken to this point, we can see how casting of actors can sometimes represent an existential dilemma. (86–87)

Whether or not readers are persuaded by Callahan's final point about the existential dilemma of casting or about the likelihood that suddenly replacing Margaret Lockwood with Madeleine Carroll would lead to the kind of Buñuelian ambiguity he describes, most of them are likely to think that he reaches that point through a series of speculations that have little to do with the scene at hand or with acting in Hitchcock or in general.

It would be pointless to criticize the rapid-fire series of gimlet-eyed observations, teasing aphorisms, and casual superlatives, positive and negative, that Callahan provides in place of a single sustained argument, for their ebullience carries his survey forward more surely than any firmly articulated argument. À *propos* of nothing in particular, for example, he observes that "Never has a movie kiss felt more richly earned and pleasurable" than the kiss Gilbert gives Iris in the back of a cab at the end of *The Lady Vanishes* (89), and that in *Sabotage*, "Mr. Verloc is perhaps the least sympathetic of all Hitchcock's villains" (75). He is even more outspoken on Hitchcock's more complex villains: "The finest or at least most vivid performance in all of Hitchcock's work seems to me to be

Robert Walker's Bruno Antony in *Strangers on a Train*" (xvii). And he goes out of his way to announce that Rod Taylor makes Mitch Brenner "the simplest and most macho guy in all of Hitchcock, even if the situations and the script tell us that he must have some issues. Put Anthony Perkins into the Mitch part and you have an entirely different film" (218).

Floating over rather than undergirding these endlessly debatable individual judgments are a more or less disconnected series of general propositions. "What Hitchcock abhorred most was complacency" (2), announces Callahan. Hitchcock was "an acting postmodernist . . . before his time" (xii) whose direction looks forward to later performances like that of Isabelle Huppert, who in her "perverse, ground zero work" in films like *The Piano Teacher* "unselfconsciously offers herself up to the camera but remains nearly wholly enigmatic" (xi–xii). Whether readers accept generalizations like these without reservation, reject them out of hand, or take them on board as subjects for further study, their enjoyment of *The Camera Lies* will depend more on individual aperçus than the generalizations Callahan intermittently derives from them.

Callahan is at his most persuasive when he focuses on specific performances and sticks to generalizations about acting that arise more naturally from them. But here his approach is even more sharply limited, as the inaccuracy of his book's title attests. His only attempt to explain this title— "The camera lies, Hitchcock would say to his actors. Not always, but sometimes"—immediately goes off on another tangent whose counter-example muddles rather than clinching his point:

> And he knew when he needed to tell as much of the truth as possible. When Hitchcock was tasked in early 1945 with editing together footage of the liberated Nazi concentration camps for a documentary, he instructed the cameramen to film as much as possible with "long tracking shots, which cannot be tampered with," according to his editor Peter Tanner. (xii)

In films that are not documentaries, what are the relations between the ways the camera lies and the ways the director of photography, the editor, the sound recordist, the composer, and of course the performer lie? This would seem to be an obvious implication of his title, but except to observe that "the camera lies and the surface is also often a lie" (xviii), Callahan never explains it further.

His subtitle, "Acting for Hitchcock," requires no explanation, but it is even less accurate than his main title, for Callahan's unsteadily focused book ignores or dismisses many Hitchcock performances and has little to say about some very important aspects of performance in general. His opening premise that "this book is an investigation of the human figure in Hitchcock's films" (xvii) is misleading, for Callahan is much more interested in performers' faces and voices than in their bodies. His observation that John Gielgud "was sometimes said to be all voice" and his recollection of Kenneth Tynan's description of him as "England's greatest actor from the neck up" (68), which he cites as a criticism of Gielgud's lack of interest in physical performance, have the unintentional effect of calling attention to the fact that Callahan himself is mostly interested in performers from the neck up. He is acutely sensitive to the variously expressive, ambiguous, and deceptive ways Hitchcock presents the faces and voices of Herbert Marshall, Joan Barry, Robert Donat, Margaret Lockwood, Michael Redgrave, Judith Anderson, Robert Walker, and Tippi Hedren. But he has remarkably little to say about the ways Cary Grant uses his body in his four very different roles for Hitchcock, and his heartfelt valentines to Ingrid Bergman are devoted almost entirely to her face and her voice. His extended discussion of *Rear Window*, which Naremore rightly singles out as a key performance text because of its insistent contrast between the understated physical performances of James Stewart and Grace Kelly and the hyperstylized performances of the largely silent neighbors they observed in long shot, focuses much more closely on the film's characters than on its performances. Callahan pauses to admire the physical performance of Peggy Ashcroft, whose "movements [in *The 39 Steps*] are slightly stagy in that she makes her physical actions decisively, underlining them a bit rather than letting them happen naturally" (65). In his most extended analysis of any single performance, he notes the way Sylvia Sidney "*very* quickly grabs the knife" (79) in the climactic dinner scene of *Sabotage* and stabs her treacherous husband below the frame line, then walks away from his corpse, her "foot trembl[ing] slightly in one of her high heel shoes" (80). Such moments are as welcome as they are rare.

Callahan properly notes that "confusing actor and character can sometimes be inevitable in movies where the character finally is the actor, or vice versa, but basic distinctions can and should be made" (17). But since he does not always distinguish sharply between performers and the characters they play, or seem to notice his failures to do so, his discussions of characters like Miss Imbrie in *Rich and Strange* sometimes feel like unwitting substitutes for the analysis of performers like Elsie Randolph, who, Callahan observes,

> convincingly plays a much older woman, and so this is a very powerful example of charged acting and casting in a Hitchcock film. He knows that if Randolph took off her glasses and put on some make-up that she would be appealing enough to partner Jack Buchanan in a musical. But Randolph's *character* in *Rich and Strange* clearly cannot do that. The glasses bring out just how long and sharp Randolph's nose is, but taking them off wouldn't do Miss Imbrie any good, partly because the personality she has developed to go with her looks is so defensively managing and flirtatious in a poisonously artificial way, and it seems as if this false personality is finally all she has become. (51)

This is almost certainly the most penetrating analysis of Miss Imbrie ever written, but it is not nearly as illuminating about Elsie Randolph. Yet the casual way Callahan shuttles back and forth between describing the character, the performance, and the performer reveals more than mere carelessness. At the heart of this highly sympathetic but apparently unfocused account are unresolved questions about the nature of performance in Hitchcock, in cinema generally, in performance texts from plays to improv to TikTok videos, and in what we like to think of as real life, the social and public life that is lived away from the gaze of the theater audience or the movie camera.

Movie actors are always acting before the camera, of course—that is what they are paid to do—but the characters they play are often acting to each other as well. It is hard to imagine a fictional narrative whose characters never assume deceptive roles within the narrative. The romantic power of the moments when Elizabeth Bennet accepts Mr. Darcy or Emma Woodhouse accepts Mr. Knightley depends on the ways Jane Austen presents them as concealing their true feelings up until that moment (in Emma's case, concealing them even from herself). Successful romantic unions in Austen's novels depend on pivotal moments in which the characters let the mask slip far enough to reveal their true attachment to one another. In the suspense thrillers Hitchcock made his specialty, characters who are guilty of crimes pile a new layer of binary distinctions (are new characters the protagonist meets innocent or guilty, sincere or deceptive, trustworthy or treacherous?) on top of the questions about performance common to all characters in all movies through their attempts to pass themselves off as innocent. So Callahan's neglect of the extensive body of performance studies that focus less anecdotally and more rigorously than he does on the relation between actors' and characters' performances is not simply an oversight but a fundamental weakness, for he never presents an equally systematic way of theorizing performance or even seems aware that such a theory might be helpful.

This neglect is all the more telling because performance is so central to Hitchcock's approach to both actors and characters. At least since Erving Goffman's influential observation that "when an individual appears in the presence of others, there will usually be some reason to mobilize his activity so that it will convey an impression to others which it is in his interests to convey," sociologists have taken a lively interest in identity as performance, not as deception, but as public self-fashioning.[5] The ubiquity of surveillance cameras, especially in Hitchcock's native land, has created a world in which it is safer to assume that we are being watched than that we are not. Even more important, the explosive rise and spread of social media has created a world in which young people in particular cultivate their public personas, like those of movie stars and politicians, with a view toward attracting as much attention as possible. Hitchcock's role in the birth of this new world of nonstop performance of everyone for everyone is prophetic, for his thrillers, individually and together, treat the binary valences of performance in thrillers (innocent or guilty? sincere or deceptive? trustworthy or treacherous?) as far more shifting, ambiguous, and open-ended than any earlier filmmaker had done. *Murder!* and *Stage Fright,* the Hitchcock films most centrally concerned with the theater, raise uncomfortable questions about the relations between Handel Fane or Charlotte Inwood's acting onstage and offstage. But these films are only the tip of Hitchcock's performance iceberg, for films from *The 39 Steps* to *Notorious* to *Rope* to *Vertigo* to *Marnie* reveal stage fright, the terror of performance coupled with a need to perform, as an existential condition.

The most typical Hitchcock performances also heighten the already ambiguous relationship between performing in a thriller, performing in the cinema, and performing oneself in real life. It is not that the performances in Hitchcock's films are more complex or nuanced or revealing or truthful than those in Hawks or Renoir or Bresson, but that they are at once subtle and obvious. The significance of every extended arm, every raised eyebrow, every vocal hesitation in a Hitchcock performance is both obvious and ambiguous. A comprehensive account of performance in Hitchcock, therefore, would embrace not only what the performers and the director do, but what the characters and the audience do as well. Callahan's frequent shifts between talking about performers and talking about the characters they play provide abundant evidence of Hitchcock's success in complicating, undermining, and deconstructing the performative conventions of the thriller, but only inferentially, not because Callahan comes out and makes this point directly himself.

This failure to theorize what is specifically Hitchcockian about Hitchcock performances is particularly regrettable because Callahan repeatedly hints at an invaluable basis for theorizing them, even if his own remarks on the subject are anecdotal and intuitive rather than systematic. His enthusiasm for the performances he loves is so great that his analyses sometimes end as rhapsodies that seek to avoid logical arguments rather than clinching them. Pausing to salute the climactic sequence in the bell tower that ends *Vertigo*, he says that "Stewart is really tremendous in this scene" and praises his stricken, self-accusing delivery of the line "You shouldn't have been that sentimental" as "really killer" (205). He pauses in his discussion of *The Paradine Case* to note that Ethel Barrymore "has a quality that is very difficult to describe, a kind of plaintive soulfulness that speaks to great understanding and great pity. It was just something Barrymore had, this quality" (149). And on Ingrid Bergman, perhaps his favorite of Hitchcock's actresses, he is more enthusiastic than eloquent:

> Bergman was such an ideal Hitchcock actress because there was an element of magic about her screen presence and also something withheld from us and maybe empty. She had a rich, musical speaking voice, the lilt of her slight Swedish accent adding force and color to her line readings, and she had a very mobile face that could seem to show everything and nothing at once. (132)

The biggest problem with impressionistic descriptions like these is not only that they sound like gushing, but that they undermine the authority of Callahan's equally impressionistic dismissals of performers who do not impress him, from Malcolm Keen and Carl Brisson in *The Manxman* to the entire cast of *Family Plot,* who "are mannered and neurotic in a way far removed from Hitchcock's earlier work" (234).

For all these reasons, *The Camera Lies* is more successful at mining a rich vein of ore about Hitchcock performances than at refining that ore into a finished product. Readers attuned to Callahan's sympathies will know that he is at his most ardently appreciative whenever he describes something as sexy, his favorite adjective. The Lodger is subjected to "a sexy crucifixion" (17). Callahan notes the "sexy shot in *Number 17* of the leading man . . . and the leading lady . . . with their hands tied to a bannister that gets even sexier when the bannister gives way and they are left hanging and swooning in space" (54). Anthony Perkins is "spindly, sexy, weird" (214) in and out of *Psycho.* Most surprisingly, Robin Wood, "one of the most insightful of all critics on Hitchcock," is "often extreme and doctrinaire in his various positions, but that was his sexy value" (227).

As this last example suggests, Callahan frequently equates sex appeal with queer appeal, a quality he celebrates in many of Hitchcock's films and delights in unmasking in others. He appreciatively notes "Novello's queer beauty" in *The Lodger* (17) and finds Joan Fontaine's pivotal scene with Judith Anderson in *Rebecca* "both ominous and queerly sexual" (104). Although many commentators have agreed that *Rope* is "a queer project from top to bottom, so to speak" (150), Callahan delights in seeking out new queer dimensions in the performances of Constance Collier, who "com[es] across as a lesbian, but this add[s] another underground queer touch" (151), and Joan Chandler, whose "delivery is highly conscious, for queer people or people in queer milieus are never naturalistic" (152). As if this were not queer enough, he adds that Francis Poulenc's *Mouvement Perpétual No. 1,* the piano tune Philip Morgan plays that provides the film's opening and closing music, "adds just the right queer culture-vulture touch" (151), and pauses to note that John Dall emphasizes Brandon Shaw's stuttering in *Rope* "in a masturbatory way" (151). When he turns to other films, Callahan calls Charles Adare in *Under Capricorn* "a queer character in every sense" (156) and thrills to "that distinctive note of absurd, queer depth" Marlene Dietrich's throwaway dialogue often sounds in *Stage Fright* (159). During Roger Thornhill's pursuit by a crop-dusting plane in *North by Northwest*, "there is a surreal quality to the images and the rhythm of the editing, and something queerly sexy, too, as Grant runs and falls to the ground and lets his torso lift in the air in his beautifully tailored gray suit" (207). Especially in his long appreciation of *Marnie*, which is "somehow the queerest of Hitchcock's films" (227) because "everything in *Marnie* is fetishized" (223), he comes close to equating Hitchcock's achievement, whether or not it involves his casting or his direction of gay performers playing straight characters or straight performers playing gay characters, with queerness, though he never quite comes out and says so.

Callahan could not be clearer in indicating his fondness for sexy moments, motifs, and performances in Hitchcock or intimating that the sexiest bits for him are the queerest. But he never indicates either why this is his own preference or what is Hitchcockian about the queerly sexy elements that so appeal to him. Plausible explanations for both these questions are easy to find. A founding principle of queer studies, another scholarly area Callahan's bibliography passes over in silence, is the ability of queering—seeing people and places and objects from a new, often forbidden angle—to raise questions about identity by revealing that they are not entirely what they seem to be.

The queerness of Hitchcock's films begins with the status most of them share as adaptations of earlier texts, for, as Pamela Demory puts it, "To adapt is to modify, to evolve, to transform, to repeat, imitate, parody, make new. To queer something is to make it strange or odd, but also to turn or transform it. To queer, then, may be to adapt; to adapt is to queer."[6] Hitchcock's cinematic adaptations of novels and plays from Oliver Sandys's *The Pleasure Garden* to Victor Canning's *The Rainbird Pattern*, which are both the same and different as the stories they adapt, destabilize the claims of the old versions to be definitive versions of these stories. An even more obvious gateway to the queerness of Hitchcock's films is performance studies, especially the analysis of self-performances by which people play public, gender, and sexual roles. The cultivation of performance in general, and the heightened awareness that we are always performing, leads to a more acute self-consciousness that queers individual identity by raising unanswerable questions about the ways it is and is not performance. In Hitchcock films especially, a heightened awareness of performance confounds the binaries on which every performance might seem to be based and perceived (public/private, male/female, gay/straight, onstage/offstage, artificial/sincere), since every performance, on or offscreen, both is and is not congruent with the performer.

Alexander Doty has noted that most commentators on queer Hitchcock "move between suggesting that queerness in Hitchcock is an inherent property of the text (whether the 'text' is Hitchcock himself or his various cultural productions) and suggesting that it takes a reader attuned to queerness, in one way or another, to explain how Hitchcock might be understood as queer."[7] Callahan faithfully replicates both these tropisms without providing a logical nexus that would link them. He is unusually sensitive to both Hitchcock's personal fascination with kinky, transgressive, or forbidden sexual practices and relationships and the endless parade of queer characters, gestures, and relationships in his films. But he never explains the relation between them in terms that would indicate the particular ways in which performance queers Hitchcock's films. Hitchcock's performers are never entirely inside or outside the characters they play for the same reason that his characters are never entirely inside or outside of the melodramatic stories in which they are caught up. Nor is Hitchcock's audience, which oscillates pleasurably between perilous immersion in his nightmare plots and the tonic withdrawal of what Hitchcock called the icebox talk, the moment for cool-headed retrospective analysis after the lights have come up.

Callahan's failure to articulate what queers so many of Hitchcock's individual performances, and Hitchcockian performance generally, is his book's single biggest disappointment. From another point of view, however, the omission of any general account of what factors or processes queer Hitchcock's cattle can be seen as not a failure but a deliberate decision to leave blank the central term in his well-illustrated but undertheorized account of acting for Hitchcock. For if what makes Hitchcock most queer is precisely his failure to commit himself to the accuracy of the familiar character types and tropes who populate his films, it seems entirely appropriate that Callahan's account of Hitchcockian performance would praise its queerness and provide abundant evidence of its queerness while leaving it up to his readers to supply the logical basis for its queerness.

Any number of Callahan's apparent digressions end up advancing his implicit argument about the pivotal importance of queer performance in Hitchcock. Just as he emphasizes the queer tension between particular characters and the familiar performers who play them, he frequently pauses to propose sharp and often surprising comparisons of films, performances, and performers that might have seemed to have little in common. Sylvia Sidney "is as subtle and nuanced in *Sabotage* as Robert Donat is in *The 39 Steps*" (73). Although James Stewart "is a fine enough actor to make a personal success out of his performance in *Rope*," Rupert Cadell, the character he plays, is finally a George Sanders part that Sanders didn't get to play" (154). "When we hear Madeleine speak [in *Vertigo*], she is like the return of Hitchcock's pseudo-British Joan Fontaine heroines of the early 1940s. . . . Madeleine and Novak exactly mimic Fontaine's breathless, precious vocal stammering, and this was carefully controlled by Hitchcock" (201). In Richard Quine's *Pushover* (1954), her first starring role, "Novak seems to hold nothing back from the camera, yet she is enigmatic, too, which makes her an ideal Hitchcock player, just as Henry Fonda was" (197).

In another series of digressions that are highly material, Callahan averts his eyes from Hitchcock's stars to focus on character performances in supporting roles, for the whole notion of a character actor capable of playing at once in and against type is as Hitchcockian as his direction of star performers whose appeal is both obvious and ambiguous. He interrupts his analysis of Handel Fane, who "can't be revealed as homosexual because this is an unspeakable and even unthinkable possibility" for the original audience of *Murder!*, by shrewdly observing that "Fane is finally less a character and more an agglomeration of increasingly unlikely occupations and attitudes" (39). He pauses over the scene in the Til Two in *Shadow of a Doubt* to single out Janet Shaw's performance as the waitress Louise Finch, Charlie Newton's ex-schoolmate, who, largely because her voice has "that hallucinatory quality that Uncle Charlie's voice has when he talks about women," is "the one character here you want to follow and know more about" (125). He contends that "Fontaine is the lead in *Rebecca,* but Anderson's Mrs. Danvers is truly the star part, the person we long to know more about" (105). So *Rebecca* is not the second Mrs. de Winter's film. It's not even the first Mrs. de Winter's film. It's a queer film that belongs to its queer heroine, Mrs. Danvers.

Hitchcock devotees who are willing to trudge through Callahan's plot summaries will find themselves endlessly provoked by a series of confident assertions that are a pleasure to argue with. Callahan's commentary is chatty, opinionated, engaging, provocative, and fun, and *The Camera Lies* will provide tonic stimulation to readers who do not insist on looking for a general theory of queer performance in Hitchcock, or are willing to accept the unspoken invitation to provide their own. For all the confidence of his remarks about particular performers and performances, Callahan has provided more questions than answers about acting in Hitchcock. To take one last marvelously queer example, he has made an unusually generous attempt to indicate a new avenue that warrants further investigation: women's coiffures, which can express characters' true natures, demarcate the roles they are playing more or less successfully, chart changes in their fortunes or personalities, or unmask them as poseurs, all the while providing centers of dazzling visual interest for his camera. In commenting on Nita Naldi's makeup for *The Mountain Eagle*, he observes that "a woman's hair would always be of the utmost importance to Hitchcock" (12). Later, comparing Mrs. Danvers's braid to that of Mrs. Sebastian in *Notorious*, he remarks, "If anything always repays close attention in Hitchcock, it is the style of women's hair and what it might tell us about them" (103). When he returns to consider Leopoldine Konstantin's work in *Notorious*, he adds parenthetically, "Always look to the hairdos in Hitchcock to find out what you need to know about a woman" (142), and later announces that Tippi Hedren's beehive hairdos make *The Birds* and *Marnie* Hitchcock's "ultimate female hair movies" (217). From the blond wigs the chorus girls wear in *The Lodger* to Johnny Aysgarth's absurd impromptu restyling of Lina Aysgarth's hair to Ann Smith's bedraggled curls after she and Jeff Custer are caught in a rainstorm while their Ferris wheel is stuck in *Mr. and Mrs. Smith* to the undoing of Maddalena Paradine's hairdo when she is jailed in *The Paradine Case* to the single curl that links Madeleine Elster to the portrait of Carlotta Valdes in *Vertigo* to the introductory closeup of Marnie washing the dye out of her hair, Hitchcock does indeed seem unusually attentive to his heroines' hairstyles as an expressive barometer, a fetish, a neglected aspect of performance that has been neglected precisely because it is rarely in the performer's control. Hitchcock scholars looking for their next project can only be grateful to Callahan for opening this particular door.

Notes

1. Both quotations are from Donald Spoto, *The Dark Side of Genius: The Life of Alfred Hitchcock* (Boston: Little, Brown, 1983), 364.

2. James Naremore, *Acting in the Cinema* (Berkeley and Los Angeles: University of California Press, 1988), 213-35, 239-61; Doug Tomlinson, "'They Should Be Treated Like Cattle': Hitchcock and the Question of Performance," in *Hitchcock's Rereleased Films: From Rope to Vertigo*, ed. Walter Raubicheck and Walter Srebnick (Detroit:

Wayne State University Press, 1991), 95-108; Susan White, "A Surface Collaboration: Hitchcock and Performance," in *A Companion to Alfred Hitchcock*, ed. Thomas Leitch and Leland Poague (Malden: Wiley-Blackwell, 2011), 181-97; Carey Martin, "The Master of Suspense and the Acrobat of the Drawing Room: How the Relationship of Cary Grant and Alfred Hitchcock Shaped Their Collaboration in *Suspicion, Notorious, To Catch a Thief,* and *North by Northwest*," *Film Journal* 12 (April 2005), online at http://works.bepress.com/carey-martin/10/; and Lesley L. Coffin, *Hitchcock's Stars: Hitchcock and the Hollywood Studio System* (Lanham: Rowman and Littlefield, 2014).

3. Quoted in Spoto, *The Dark Side of Genius*, 406.

4. François Truffaut, with the assistance of Helen Scott. *Hitchcock*. Rev. ed. (New York: Simon and Schuster, 1983), 73.

5. Erving Goffman, *The Presentation of Self in Everyday Life* (Garden City: Doubleday Anchor, 1959), 4.

6. Pamela Demory, "Queer/Adaptation: An Introduction," in *Queer/Adaptation: A Collection of Critical Essays*, ed. Pamela Demory (New York: Palgrave Macmillan, 2019), 1.

7. Alexander Doty, "Queer Hitchcock," in *A Companion to Alfred Hitchcock*, 473.

John Bruns

The Dark Comedy Side of Genius

Wes D. Gehring, *Hitchcock and Humor: Modes of Comedy in Twelve Defining Films*. Jefferson, NC: McFarland and Company, 2019. 290 pp. $39.95 paperback.

> The wise man laughs only with fear and trembling.
> – Baudelaire, "Of the Essence of Laughter, and generally of the Comic in the Plastic Arts"[1]

In the early summer of 1954, Alfred Hitchcock was on location in France's Côte d'Azur, specifically Nice's Marché des Fleurs, shooting a scene from *To Catch a Thief* (1955). The occasion presented film critic André Bazin the perfect opportunity either to confirm or refute the claims coming from a growing cabal of Hitchcock fanatics—including Maurice Scherer (soon to be known as Eric Rohmer), Alexandre Astruc, Jacques Rivette, and François Truffaut— about the "flawless genius" of the director. Far more open-minded than closed, Bazin was willing to see his published reservations about Hitchcock's recent films—*The Paradine Case* (1947), *Rope* (1948), and *I Confess* (1950)—"reduced to rubble" (140).[2]

In his interview with Hitchcock, published in the October 1954 issue of *Cahiers du cinéma* as "Hitchcock *contre* Hitchcock," Bazin asked the director to discuss the "unity" of his work. Hitchcock demurred somewhat, saying he preferred to think that what he was after as a director was for everything to go his "way." When pressed to elaborate, the director "spoke of a certain relationship between drama and comedy," writes Bazin. "The only films that may be taken as 'pure Hitchcock' are those in which he has been able to play with this discordant relationship." Bazin's pursuit of this line of questioning paid off, as it revealed an aspect central to Hitchcock's style—an aspect that, even today, remains under-examined: humor. "I risked the word," writes Bazin. "Hitchcock accepts it; what he is trying to express may well be taken as a form of humor and he spontaneously cites *The Lady Vanishes* as conforming most closely to his ideal."[3]

As with so many things regarding the cinema, Bazin was way ahead of us all.

With his recent book, *Hitchcock and Humor: Modes of Comedy in Twelve Defining Films*, Wes Gehring hopes to play catch-up. The author of well over a dozen film books, including *Buster Keaton in His Own Time: What the Responses of 1920s Critics Reveal, Irene Dunne: First Lady of Hollywood,* and *Romantic vs. Screwball Comedy: Charting the Difference,* Gehring now gives us the most sustained and thorough examination of humor in Hitchcock to date.[4] Given Bazin's conclusion that the director's British films were more humorous and therefore more purely Hitchcockian, one might guess that the majority of the twelve "defining" films Gehring has selected are British. But the book tilts toward the American films, with individual chapters devoted to *Mr. and Mrs. Smith* (1941); what the author calls Hitchcock's "Nietzschean Dark Comedy Trilogy" of *Shadow of a Doubt* (1943), *Rope* (1948), and *Strangers on a Train* (1951); *Rear Window* (1954); then *The Trouble with Harry* (1955); and *North by Northwest* (1959). Including a brief epilogue devoted to *Psycho* (1960), that's eight American films to Britain's five: *Blackmail* (1929), *The Man Who Knew Too Much* (1934), *The 39 Steps* (1935), *Secret Agent* (1936), and that purest of Hitchcocks, *The Lady Vanishes* (1938).

Gehring's book dismisses outright (and rightly) the idea of "comic relief"—a reductive formula that short-shrifts the force and reach of comedy and, at the same time, serves to reinforce cultural and academic attitudes that only sober matters are worthy of critical attention. In film writing, the idea of comic relief seems nowhere near as harmful as the latter proposition suggests. But consider this review of

Drumline (dir. Charles Stone III, 2002): "Devon's romantic interest in a cheerleader (Zoë Saldana) provides a few tender moments; references to his troubled family background lend a touch of pathos; and a cast of stock secondary characters is on hand for occasional comic relief."[5] Harmless, right? Perhaps. But note the sly implications here: comedy is "secondary" (or in this case, a mere show, with "tender moments" winning and "pathos" placing). Such is our shared, automatic thinking—or non-thinking—when it comes to comedy. The idea of comic relief contains the power of comedy, a power that Hitchcock unleashed consistently throughout his five-decade-long career. Or as Gehring puts it, "the pieces of humor which surface so consistently and casually in Hitchcock's films are much more than mere random distractions. Indeed, the director's brew is most broad" (60). Call this concoction of drama and comedy "Hitch's brew."

For Gehring, and for others who take Hitchcock's comedy seriously, it is not a sideshow, a temporary distraction from the deadly serious matters at hand (a sexual assault in *Blackmail*, a child-kidnapping in *The Man Who Knew Too Much*, a would-be perfect murder in *Rope*, and so on), but a way of conceiving such matters, a way of situating them, and a way of making sense of them. Indeed, the trivialization of comedy is surely related to the fear that comedy will tell us something we don't want to hear. More like Cordelia than the Fool in *King Lear*, it is the candor of comedy we cannot bear, or even understand. Mark Hennelly, Jr., astutely wrote of Hitchcock's sense of the carnivalesque which, following Bakhtin, can be understood to privilege ambivalence over certainty as its worldview. Thus, one may trace the ways in which Hitchcock's films provoke us "to see and sympathize differently or otherwise than usual, that is, according to the traditional wisdom of carnival alterity."[6] Readers may think here of *The Ring* (1927) or the fairground sequences in *Strangers on a Train*, in which Hitchcock's camera wanders through a topsy-turvy world of danger and delight, and it is the literal carnival in Hitchcock's films that concerns

Hennelly. But broadly speaking, Hitchcock's sense of the *carnivalesque* is revealed not just in specific set pieces but in numerous Hitchcockian tropes. As David Sterritt has observed, "Hitchcock uses doubling to explore characteristic 'Hitchcockian' themes, particularly the ambiguity of good and evil and the transference of guilt and innocence. In the uncertainty, instability, and ambivalence that they evoke, such themes are clearly carnivalistic, especially when juxtaposed with the certainties of more formulaic specimens of Hollywood cinema."[7]

Thus, both Hennelly and Sterritt employ the term *carnival* in different though related ways. Other critics who break down Hitch's brew of drama and comedy operate with different terminology altogether: for Thomas M. Leitch, the operative terms are "games" and "play"—or what John W. Roberts elsewhere calls Hitchcock's "ludic style."[8] For Susan Smith and James Naremore, the operative term is "humor"; for Richard Allen, it's "romantic irony," for Lesley Brill, "redemptive comedy," for Jack Sullivan, "lethal laughter," and so on.[9] And while Gehring himself employs many of these terms, it's Hitchcock's "dark comedy" that emerges as the most crucial. As Hitchcock himself put it, "All my films are dark comedies" (qtd. in Gehring 3).

Hitchcock's contemporary audience seemed to understand this, as demonstrated by the plethora of contemporaneous reviews Gehring provides (*The New York World-Telegram*'s description of *The 39 Steps* is "an excellent amalgamation of humor and melodrama"; the *New York Times* doesn't know whether to call *The Lady Vanishes* a "brilliant melodrama" or a "brilliant comedy"; the *Christian Science Monitor* complains of too much "smoking car humor" in *Rear Window*). The reviews Gehring cites allow us to appreciate more fully not just how much the world viewed Hitchcock comically but, more importantly, just how much Hitchcock viewed the world comically. That is, for Hitchcock, comedy is a credo: it's that "way" of doing things to which he alluded in his conversation with Bazin on the set of *To Catch a Thief*. Were we to ask Hitchcock why he filled *Psycho* with so much dark comedy, for example, we might imagine he would respond, Mandalorian-like, "This is the way."

While "dark comedy" is the principal concern of *Hitchcock and Humor*, Gehring's book also focuses, though not equally, on three sub-genres: personality comedy, screwball comedy, and what Gehring calls "parody of reaffirmation," a concept the author first explored in a previous work.[10] Whereas a conventional parody might skewer a particular film genre just for laughs, as Mel Brooks's *Blazing Saddles* (1974) does to the Western, the "parody of reaffirmation" treats its target with more respect, to the point where the film is as much parody as it is poignant tribute. Gehring makes no claims that Hitchcock was well-versed in each of these comedy sub-genres, only that "he was instinctually drawn to them" (26). The first and second sub-genres dominate the first several chapters, as Gehring gives what for some Hitchcock fans may be a long-awaited study of Peter Lorre's performances in *The Man Who Knew Too Much* and *Secret Agent*. The recent émigré's portrayal of the anarchist Abbott in the former film draws parodically from Paul Muni's titular anti-hero in *Scarface* (dir. Howard Hawks, 1933) and from the conventions of the gangster film as a whole. In a clever move, courtesy of a helpful quotation from Robin Wood, Gehring notes that Lorre's Abbott is, like Muni's Scarface, child-like and sympathetic, more clown than butcher. Lorre's portrayal of the Mexican secret agent of *Secret Agent*, known simply as The General, draws in large part from Harpo Marx—a comic touch not lost on contemporary audiences, as the reviews Gehring provides show. One review not quoted by Gehring supports his appreciative comments on Lorre in the two Hitchcock films, Graham Greene's "The Genius of Peter Lorre" (published in *World Film News* in July 1936).

Naturally Gehring doesn't wait until the chapter devoted to *Mr. and Mrs. Smith* before he elaborates upon the many screwball moments in Hitchcock's films, and he rightly situates many of Hitchcock's British films within the sphere of the genre's influence. Arguably the greatest of them all, *The 39 Steps* was released at the peak of the screwball's popularity:

just after Hawks's *Twentieth Century* (1934) and Capra's *It Happened One Night* (1934), and before Gregory La Cava's *My Man Godfrey* (1936) and Leo McCarey's *The Awful Truth* (1937). In fact, it is Capra's film that *The 39 Steps* "often resembles," says Gehring, with the romantic coupling of its clownish duo, Hannay (Robert Donat) and Pamela (Madeleine Carroll), occurring on the road, as it did with Peter Warne (Clark Gable) and Ellie Andrews (Claudette Colbert) (63). While Gehring isn't the first to note the influence of the screwball on Hitchcock during his late British period (Thomas Schatz makes a similar observation, singling out *The 39 Steps* and *The Lady Vanishes* in particular), he shows that it is much more than a side note.[11]

Not surprisingly, the comedy genres Gehring examines are not discrete. For instance, Gehring's interpretation of the screwball comedy is inflected with darkly comic elements. While many scholars take it as a given that the romantic coupling in a screwball follows the patterns of Old Comedy, in which the marriage fulfills a promise of social integration and renewal, Gehring can't seem to shake the feeling that the marriage is doomed. This, it turns out, is one of the most engaging and provocative ideas in the book: that in Hitchcock and elsewhere (but in Hitchcock especially) marriage drains love from a relationship (126). This is not to say that critics have not articulated the ways the screwball comedy mystifies romance in order to do some essential cultural work, but Gehring's analysis of marriage in Hitchcock is not ideological.[12] Instead, Gehring traces Hitchcock's critique of the institution of marriage to the filmmaker's own personal predilections. For Gehring, "dark comedy remains Hitchcock's core," and so everything is inflected with it, including his views toward holy matrimony (20). For *Rear Window*, Gehring gives "the duration of any Lisa-Jeff relationship the time it takes for two broken legs to heal" (209). Not surprisingly, Gehring is pessimistic about *To Catch a Thief*'s "seemingly simpatico ending," given that it is punctuated by Frances's casual line about mother living with them (36). As for *North by Northwest*, while Gehring acknowledges our desire for Roger and Eve to enjoy a long-term partnership, "tradition makes it a thumbs down future for the duo" (247).

The darkly comic vision at Hitchcock's "core" begins with *Blackmail*, and Gehring devotes the first two chapters of the book to Hitchcock's first sound film: a prologue entitled "Working Toward *Blackmail*," followed by a chapter devoted to what he calls the "the most definite of dark comedies" (27). While readers will appreciate Gehring for calling Crewe's actions attempted rape (rather than, say, a "forcible embrace"), he doesn't quite articulate just how we are to align the artist Crewe's attempted rape of Alice, which is at the center of the film's story, with Hitchcock's darkly comic view.[13] Gehring does state that "in dark comedy, sex and death have long been associated as a loss of control—a sense of life's chaos," but the idea isn't developed (33). It would have been interesting for Gehring to consider how *Blackmail* might fit within the tradition of New Comedy, particularly those plays (Plautus's *Truculentus* and Terence's *Hecyra*, for instance) in which wild, religious festivals lead to rape. The moments in the artist's loft leading up to Crewe's attempted rape suggest a kind of mini-Bacchanal: music and song, drink, livery, etc. The resulting chaos has echoes throughout Hitchcock, culminating, most clearly, in the murder scene at the Magic Isle in *Strangers on a Train*. Such lines of thought would paint an even darker portrait of Hitchcock's comic worldview.

Early on, Gehring establishes that Hitchcock's dark humor is rooted in what he calls the duality of artist/adolescent—the childish impulses that the master filmmaker expressed in his films, as well as in the lewd jokes he enjoyed on and off the set, e.g., his habit of introducing himself as "Hitch, no cock" (119). Gehring proposes "to take that same artists/adolescent Doppler effect and direct it at various forms of humor" (9). Twice Gehring presents us with quotations from Hitchcock that reveal the director's fondness for breaking china—even on set. But readers may sense a missed opportunity: the anecdotes, taken together, call for a reconsideration of the scene from *The Birds* in which Lydia crawls on the floor of the Brenner house in a pointless effort to clean up broken teacups, while a curious Melanie looks on. There's some cruel irony to all of this when, in a later scene, just prior to her grisly discovery of Dan Fawcett's corpse, Lydia notices broken teacups in the dead farmer's kitchen. Is this another one of Hitchcock's many private jokes that Gehring suggests the director inserted into his films for his own amusement? It's a pity that the 1963 film gets virtually no attention here, especially in light of the author's emphasis on the screwball elements of Hitchcock's films. The first thirty minutes of *The Birds* is steeped in that tradition (something that both Hitchcock and screenwriter Evan Hunter said they had in mind for the first part of *The Birds*).[14] And any film that gives screen time to Richard Deacon *must* be a comedy—he's as fine an example of what Gehring calls "personality comedy" as there is. But as with any good work, and Gehring's book surely is that, curious readers will be inspired to add to it their examples and illustrations, encouraged, even, to drift temporarily from the page altogether in order to indulge other possibilities.

The real strength of Gehring's book is the way it zeroes in on moments when fear and trembling spill into laughter and vice versa, such as when in *The Lady Vanishes* the hapless duo of Caldicott and Chalmers (to whom the author devotes several pages) quite unexpectedly become quite brave—and useful—during the final, and very serious, shootout. Or when in *Secret Agent* Ashenden and the General, in search of their church connection, are struck by the ominous sound of a single organ chord: "Further explanation finds their church connection dead at the organ. While Gielgud's Ashenden is bothered by the murder, Lorre comically mimes the slitting of a throat, while he professionally admires the murderer's craftmanship" (82-83).

Gehring has a breezy and playful writing style. I found myself chuckling aloud at times. His prose is also, at times, wickedly cynical, as for example when he refers to the kidnapped Betty in the 1934 version of *The Man Who Knew Too Much* as "a losable daughter" (49). It's jabs such as this that readers may find unnecessary, since Gehring doesn't elaborate. His snarky description of Betty is likely to make readers think of other moments in Hitchcock that feature an annoying child—such as the little pest on the tube who repeatedly harasses a bookish Hitchcock in his requisite cameo in *Blackmail;* or the noisy young boy playing cowboy in *Strangers on a Train,* whose balloon Bruno pops with a lit cigarette; or the snotty little Jessie Cotton in *Marnie* (1964), whose whiny demands of Bernice Edgar, "How 'bout mah pie? How 'bout mah pecan pie?" grate on the viewer's nerves. Indeed, there is something about the way Hitchcock attacks the sanctity of the child in a darkly comic way; and given Gehring's extended thoughts about Hitchcock's cynical attitude toward marriage, the absence of any discussion of the annoying Hitchcock child seems a missed opportunity.[15]

Yet the book really sputters when Gehring feels compelled to remind us of the many instances in which critics have ignored or downplayed the comic elements in Hitchcock's films. A few examples: "Too often anything funny in his films other than black humor have been dismissed as comic relief" (1); "Thus never let Hitchcock, or any cinema critic, pass off moments like this scene in [*The 39*] *Steps* as only comic relief" (68); "While critics often reference a Hitchcock film as a 'melodramatic thriller,' and the director was most apt to call his films 'dark comedies,' *Secret Agent* begs to be called a hybrid comedy" (78); "Why all the fuss? Because one simply tires of everything being lumped unceremoniously together into something minimized as mere 'Hitchcock comic relief'" (223). Nearly all of his claims of critical misrepresentation are not backed up with references (who are these critics? where does one find them?). It's an unnecessary rhetorical move on Gehring's part to insist that some serious wrongs need righting (indeed, "Why all the fuss?"). The book's true aim isn't to set the record straight, but simply to set the record—in this case, for the most thorough and sustained analysis of comedy in Hitchcock.

This compulsion to harp on the oversights of other critics extends to at least one other area of Hitchcock studies:

Hitchcock and adaptation. In his chapter on *Secret Agent*, Gehring claims that "previous Hitchcock studies have been dismissive of the influence of Maugham's stories" (81). None of these previous Hitchcock studies are cited, and the first study of this subject that comes to my mind, R. Barton Palmer's "*Secret Agent*: Coming in from the Cold, Maugham Style," is hardly dismissive of Maugham's influence.[16] The compulsion spreads to the book's subsequent chapter on *The Lady Vanishes*. Gehring laments that (once again unnamed) Hitchcock "historians" (his quotation marks) treat the film's source novel, Ethel Lina White's *The Wheel Spins*, unjustly by saying it lacks "farcical elements"—yet I found Noel King and Toby Miller's essay, "*The Lady Vanishes* but She Won't Go Away" not guilty of this crime.[17] Curiously, Gehring claims the "historians" will *never* do the novel justice, which seems to undercut the purpose (and success) of *Hitchcock and Humor*, which is to raise readers' awareness of numerous things, among them the farcical elements of White's novel. Worse, Gehring's research into contemporaneous critics may strike readers as a way of bypassing more demanding scholarly discussions.

Which brings me to the book's main weakness, which is the absence of acknowledgment of the critical work already done in this area—much of it from the past thirty years or so. Consider this passage from Gehring's chapter on *Mr. and Mrs. Smith*: "Ever since forever, *Mr. and Mrs. Smith*, Alfred Hitchcock's first set-in-America film, has been treated like an aberration in the director's filmography—seen simply as a mere screwball/farce past its heyday, and seemingly at odds with today's Hitchcock's auteur image of suspense and horror. One can hear some condescending cinema snob flippantly observing, 'Well, even Edward Hopper . . . had Monday mornings'" (114). Fair enough. But some advice to Gehring would be to stop listening to condescending cinema snobs, real or imagined. In his fine essay, "The Light Side of Genius: Hitchcock's *Mr. and Mrs. Smith* in the Screwball Tradition," Dana Polan explores what it means "to treat *Mr. and Mrs. Smith* as a Hitchcock film *while treating it as a screwball comedy and as part of the Hollywood system"* (emphasis in original).[18] Taking Polan's approach into account rather than overlooking it would surely support Gehring's effort to align the screwball with the darker forces at work in Hitchcock, particularly if we consider, as Gehring smartly does, the murderous impulses of Carol Lombard's Mrs. Smith toward her husband: "How great a leap is it from a ha-ha screwball world to that of existentialistic black humor—in which a certain knowledge of what is right or wrong is missing?" (124).

Susan Smith offers up what may seem to be the very kind of dismissal of the comic in Hitchcock against which Gehring rails when she raises the question of "why Hitchcock's more uncharacteristic, off-beat attempts at comedy either fail to work very well (as in the case of *Mr. and Mrs. Smith*, his sole venture into screwball) or (as with *The Trouble with Harry*, his pastoral black comedy) lack the usual sense of tension and complexity."[19] Yet her larger argument comes very close to Gehring's. Making a counterintuitive move Gehring might praise, Smith argues that *Sabotage* (1936) is a better example of the comic than *Mr. and Mrs. Smith*, insofar as the former strikes the right balance between fear and laughter—precisely the "pure Hitchcock" Bazin distilled from his conversation with the director that sunny French afternoon back in 1954.

And like Gehring, Smith has Hitchcock on her side here. Take a quick glance at the index of *Alfred Hitchcock: Interviews*, edited by Sidney Gottlieb, and you'll see references to comedy, humor, and jokes alongside references to fear and violence. Here's Hitchcock speaking to Janet Maslin in 1972: "To me, *Psycho* was a big comedy. Had to be."[20] *Had to be*? Yes, because Hitchcock understood screams to be a blood relative of laughter. And here's Hitchcock speaking to Oriana Fallaci in 1963: "Now take an adolescent on a roller coaster. Why does he ride the roller coaster? Because every bend, every drop, fills him with horror, and this is fun."[21]

In this way, Hitchcock expands and reverses Baudelaire's axiom that I use as my epigraph: we all fear and tremble only with laughter. Here I'm thinking of William Paul's anecdote about the audience's reaction to the ending of *Carrie* (1976), directed by Brian De Palma (a prolific disciple of Hitchcock). At the very end of the film, the character Sue (Amy Irving) visits the grave of Carrie (Sissy Spacek) to pay her respects. The serene scene is a welcoming and much-needed ending after the hellfire roller coaster that is the film's climax. But just as Sue places a bouquet near Carrie's defiled tombstone, an arm suddenly reaches up from the earth and grabs her. According to Paul, and as De Palma no doubt hoped, the audience broke into a collective scream, followed by a sustained and collective buzz as the lights went up and the curtain closed. Writes Paul, "as we walked out of the theater, the buzz initiated by the scream segued into laughter."[22]

And while Paul's focus is on the pleasure of resolution giving way to irresolution (one of the key features of comedy, as I argue elsewhere), one can't help but think of Hitchcock's roller coaster analogy.[23] Surely *Psycho*'s audience reacted similarly when Lila's discovery of a (seemingly) reposed Mrs. Bates is followed quickly by a one-two punch: first the grisly reveal, then the knife-wielding Norman-in-drag. I often wonder if audiences were even paying attention to the psychobabble of the film's coda, if they were instead reveling in the same collective buzz-cum-laughter that Paul describes. The sequence from *Sabotage* in which the London movie-going crowd reacts to the city-wide power outage, first with panic and confusion, then with collective laughter, perfectly demonstrates Hitchcock's awareness early on of his audience's appetite for thrills and spills.

With dark comedy, as well as personality comedy, screwball comedy, and "parody of reaffirmation," the author's plate is full enough. But one could certainly add a side dish of physical comedy, for Hitchcock often reveled in exploiting the sheer silliness of bodies—especially male bodies. Indeed, what seems to be something of a constant in Hitchcock is his depiction of male clumsiness (a trope that suits Gehring's focus on what he says is a key aspect of dark comedy: "man as beast"). In a Chaplinesque moment from *Rich and Strange* (1931), Fred Hill (Henry Kendall) tries to maintain balance on a crowded tube train by grabbing the feathers of an elderly woman's hat. Feigning poise, he proceeds to open a large newspaper, sending it flapping into the face of the man standing next to him. The sheets begin to spill from Fred's grasp, and he struggles to gather them together (from a shapeless mass of crumpled newspaper, an advertisement stares back up at him: "Are you satisfied with your present Circumstances?") In addition to the slapstick silliness at Ambrose Chappell's taxidermy shop in the 1956 remake of *The Man Who Knew Too Much*, consider the amount of attention Hitchcock gives to Ben Conway (James Stewart) as he struggles with traditional Bedouin seating, beginning with the close-up of Jill Conway (Doris Day) gazing up worriedly through her husband's gangly ostrich legs. A similarly comic scene can be found in *Under Capricorn* (1949), when Charles Adare (Michael Wilding), sherry in hand, steps awkwardly between Mr. Banks (Bill Shine) and the governor (Cecil Parker), who is bathing in a comically-too-small tub.

And physical humor is not limited to the less-than-suave male. Think of the scene in *The 39 Steps* in which the hand-cuffed couple, Hannay and Pamela, find themselves sharing a single room at a countryside inn. Hannay's right hand slaps wildly about, fish-like, as Pamela hungrily eats a sandwich, only to land rather uncouthly on her knee. In *The 39 Steps*-like *Saboteur* (1942), the upright Barry Kane (Robert Cummings) attempts to escape the Tobin Ranch on horseback, only to be chased down by a cowboy who lassoes him to the dirt as if he were a calf in a rodeo competition. There's a bit of comic theater at the Baccarat table in *To Catch a Thief* (1955), when the very suave John Robie (Cary Grant) accidentally/deliberately drops his 10,000 *francs plaque* down the front of a lady's dress. Robie does his best to make it an exquisitely embarrassing scene, all for the amusement of the bejeweled Jessie Stevens (Jessie Royce Landis). Moments before this, an elegantly dressed Robie wreaks havoc in the flower market as he tries to elude two French detectives, diving headlong into a colorful display of carnations. An angry flower shop owner whacks him over the head repeatedly with a bouquet of white tuberoses. Robie manages to escape, but not for long. Seconds later, the same old woman grabs hold of Robie's sleeve as he runs behind a tree, making it seem that his left arm is orbiting impossibly (or "Stretch Armstrong"-like) around its trunk.

But it's the hapless cop who is most often the butt of the joke in Hitchcock, beginning perhaps with policeman Joe (Malcolm Keen) in *The Lodger* (1926). And the Hitchcock cop is not exempt from exhibiting bodily goofiness either. There's Detective Tom Doyle (Wendell Corey) splashing brandy down the front of his suit, undercutting his smug and knowing dismissal of Lisa (Grace Kelly) and Jeff (James Stewart), who rightly suspect that Lars Thorwald is guilty of murder. The cartoonish nightmare sequence from the otherwise austere *Vertigo* (1958) has never failed to elicit snickers from my students, especially the disembodied head of Detective Scottie Ferguson (James Stewart) hurtling through space, with his small, quivering toss of hair. And I'm sure Gehring would agree that it's a guilty pleasure to chuckle as Detective Arbogast (Martin Balsam) takes his backwards fall down the stairs inside the Bates house in *Psycho* (1960). All the more reason for Hitchcock to punctuate the pratfall with the sickening plunge of Norman's knife into Arbogast's chest. Among the many wonderful Hitchcock quotations Gehring has dug up, this one nearly tops them all, and is relevant here: Hitchcock tells a reporter that he had an idea "of opening a film with a half-dozen Keystone Kops crawling out of a tunnel, while a thug stands over the exit with a club and hits each one coming out. Wouldn't it be interesting to show a close-up [of the sixth cop] with blood trickling down his face—comedy suddenly turned sober" (15).

One way to think about the comedy of the male body in Hitchcock is in terms of Henri Bergson's idea of "elasticity," or the sudden transformation of the body. That is, we laugh not *at* poor Arbogast, but at the sudden change of his body. In fact, argues Bergson, it is the change itself that is the source of laughter. Climbing the stairs, with cautious confidence, Arbogast's body is a figure of a dry, clinical police procedural—bringing to mind what Bergson refers to as the "mechanization" of the human body: all business. The sudden and shocking appearance of Mrs. Bates jolts his body out of mere automatism and rigidity into a kind of rubbery disequilibrium. Importantly, Truffaut says that he is grateful to Bazin for "using the key word 'equilibrium' in connection with Hitchcock."[24] And while Bazin may have used that word in conversation with Truffaut, in print Bazin actually used the key word "*dis*equilibrium."[25] As I note elsewhere, Bazin spoke of a *mise-en-scène* in Hitchcock that shows "reality only in those moments when a plumb line dropped from the dramatic center of gravity is about to leave the supporting polygon, scorning the initial commotion as well as the fracas of the fall."[26] Truffaut's recollection regarding equilibrium is that Bazin was likely referring to Hitchcock's lifelong fear, due to his weight, of losing his balance. Perhaps . . . though it is just as likely that Bazin was putting his finger on just what is so darkly comic in Hitchcock, and here one cannot help but think of a scene out of the 1932 short, *The Music Box* by Laurel and Hardy (a comic duo referenced lovingly and frequently in Gehring's book): "a disequilibrium comparable to that of a heavy mass of steel beginning to slide down too sharp an incline, about which one could easily calculate the future acceleration."

That a discussion of physical comedy in Hitchcock is largely absent from *Hitchcock's Humor* hardly diminishes the book's importance. Readers will benefit from an abundance of wonderful moments, such as the last few pages of the chapter on *Mr. and Mrs. Smith*, which draws heavily on Gehring's knowledge of both screwball comedy and the life of Carole Lombard.[27] The chapter on *Shadow of a Doubt* is quite strong, although it distracts a bit with some errors, as when Gehring says the inscription on the ring Uncle Charlie gives to his niece reads "from T.S. to B.M." The inscription is actually "T.S. from B.M," so Gehring's suggestion that Thelma Schenley (the T.S.) gave Bruce Matthewson (the B.M.) the ring (rather than the other way around) isn't convincing. More convincing, or at least more interesting, is Gehring's hypothesis (which again invokes the artist/adolescent duality) that the lettering is a scatological joke, courtesy of a very naughty Hitchcock: "T.S."

stands for "total shit" and "B.M" stands for "bowel movement." This certainly would suit Uncle Charlie's worldview, which is that the world is a "foul sty." Further, it is a worldview worth inscribing in stone, lest one forget it (the advice Uncle Charlie gives to his niece at the 'Til-Two club is to "wake up" and face this harsh truth). All the more reason for Gehring to get the inscription correct, as "[T]otal [S]hit from [B]owel [M]ovement" is just too darkly comic to waste.

Another distraction in the *Shadow* chapter is that Gehring treats Joe Newton (Henry Travers) and his partner in would-be crime Herb (Hume Cronyn) a bit harshly. Gehring considers them stupid and oblivious to the danger Uncle Charlie poses: "Joe and Herbie [*sic*] *never* realize the truth, let alone protect Young Charlie from her murdering uncle. Joe and Herbie remain stupid squared throughout" (148). Well, isn't everyone in Santa Rosa but Charlie (and perhaps Ann) oblivious to the danger Uncle Charlie poses?[28] Also, Herb does save Charlie's life: he hears her cries from the garage in which Uncle Charlie has trapped her, with the car running and no key to switch it off as it belches poisonous exhaust. "She might have died. You saved her. You knew just what to do," Emma (Patricia Collinge) tells her brother. We know better, of course, and Herb isn't too shy to boast a little about his role in the rescue: "Don't know how I came across her." Inadvertent heroism, to be sure, but heroism, nonetheless. And this is just the kind of dark comedy that typifies Hitchcock: what rotten luck for Uncle Charlie! His plan to murder his knowing niece is foiled—and by Herb, of all people!

But the real injustice may be the false charge Gehring lays on Emma: that she henpecks Joe. She does not. If anything, she is guilty of sidelining Joe altogether so she can freely dote on her younger brother. And it's a shame that Emma doesn't get more attention in this chapter, as she is one of the more delightfully comic figures in Hitchcock's *oeuvre*. One might say that Emma is a direct descendent of the wonderfully dopey Miss Bates from the Jane Austen novel that shares her name. Consider this innocuous moment during the party in Uncle Charlie's honor, when Emma presents a tray full of sandwiches to one of the guests. Just as the guest reaches for a sample, Emma stops her and says, "Not that one. Why'd I make tomato? They always soak through the bread. Try one of these. It's whole wheat bread and cream cheese. It's the paprika makes it pink!" Hearing Collinge playfully deliver that last line is one of the film's many great joys. And Emma is a deeply sympathetic character, so one can only wonder from whence this silly sandwich snafu stems. The image of red tomato soaking through white bread conjures up all sorts of possibilities, not least of which is the idea of Emma's repressed desire, a longing for her youth and single status that she can barely disguise.[29] It's a possibility that well suits Gehring's argument that Hitchcock's comedy is infused with a critical (and comical) attitude toward marriage—an idea he pursues with aplomb throughout the book.[30]

There are a few lines Gehring devotes to Emma that are worth noting: Emma shares with her eldest daughter a (rare) photograph of Charlie as a young boy, taken the day of the bicycle accident that fractured his skull. Like Ann, the young boy was an avid reader. But the accident changed all that (for the worse). "When the pictures came home, how mama cried," Emma recalls, "she wondered if he'd ever be the same." To which Gehring cuttingly adds, "Gosh, do you think Emma and Charlie's mom was onto something? Plus, Emma tells her long tale in front of the whole family, including future Uncle 'Killer' Charlie" (150). Never mind that only the two Charlies are present, because Gehring's point is that this scene is pulled right out of Hitchcock's "down-on-humanity bag of tricks" (149). It is true that the macabre backstory Emma recounts is close to "laugh out loud" funny (150). And it's all-the-more darkly comic if we have taken note of a small detail that occurs during the scene of Emma and her younger brother's reunion, earlier in the film. As Emma emerges from the Newton house to greet her younger brother, Uncle Charlie stops her. "Emma, don't move. Standing there, you don't look like Emma Newton. You look like Emma Spenser Oakley of 46 Burnham Street, St. Paul, Minnesota, the prettiest girl on the block!" Just as he utters these words, dripping with nostalgia for halcyon days, we see in the background a young boy speeding down the street on a bicycle.

Gehring ends *Hitchcock and Humor* on a somewhat modest note, asking readers to "further widen and appreciate" the crack in the door he has opened. "Hitchcock was not unlike the neglected scholarly humorist Richard Armour, who was fond of saying he '. . . wore two outfits— cap and gown and cap and bells.' Thus, look beyond the Hitchcock thrills . . . and his English undertaker's garb. The cap and bells are there too" (253). And perhaps one of the lasting, albeit inadvertent, benefits of Gehring's book is that readers will indeed further widen the crack in the door and find, inside, Richard Allen, Lesley Brill, Mark Hennelly Jr., Thomas Leitch, James Naremore, Susan Smith, Dana Polan, John W. Roberts, David Sterritt, Jack Sullivan, and others. With Bazin playing host.

Notes

1. Charles Baudelaire, "Of the Essence of Laughter, and generally of the Comic in the Plastic Arts," in *Selected Writings on Art and Literature*, trans. P.E. Charvet (New York: Penguin Classics, 1993), 141.

2. André Bazin, *The Cinema of Cruelty: From Buñuel to Hitchcock* (New York: Arcade Publishing, 1982), 147. Originally published in 1975 by Editions Flammarion, Paris, as *Le Cinéma de la Cruauté*. One should bear in mind that in 1954 these films were, to French moviegoers, more recent than their American release dates suggest because of their delayed release in France. It may be time to give Bazin's writings on Hitchcock fuller reconsideration, beginning with this posthumous collection.

3. Bazin, *The Cinema of Cruelty*, 147.

4. Wes D. Gehring, *Buster Keaton in His Own Time: What the Responses of 1920s Critics Reveal* (Jefferson, North Carolina: McFarland, 2018); *Irene Dunne: First Lady of Hollywood* (Lanham, MD: Scarecrow Press, 2006); and *Romantic vs. Screwball Comedy: Charting the Difference* (Lanham, MD: Scarecrow Press, 2008).

5. A.O. Scott, "A Rousing Halftime Show Bigger Than the Game," *New York Times*, 13 December 2002, 35.

6. Mark Hennelly, Jr., "Hitchcock's Carnival," *Hitchcock Annual* 13 (2008), 155.

7. David Sterritt, "The Diabolic Imagination: Hitchcock, Bakhtin, and the Carnivalization of Cinema," *Hitchcock Annual* 1 (1998), 106.

8. See Thomas M. Leitch, *Find the Director and Other Hitchcock Games* (Athens: University of Georgia, 1991), and John R. Roberts, "From Hidden Pictures to Productive Pictures: Hitchcock's Ludic Style," *Hitchcock Annual* 19 (2014): 181-207.

9. See Susan Smith, *Hitchcock: Suspense, Humour and Tone* (London: BFI, 2000); James Naremore, "Hitchcock and Humor," *Strategies: Journal of Theory, Culture & Politics* 14, no. 1 (2001), 13-25; Richard Allen, *Hitchcock's Romantic Irony* (New York: Columbia University Press, 2007); Lesley Brill, "Redemptive Comedy in the Films of Alfred Hitchcock and Preston Sturges: 'Are Snakes Necessary?,'" in *Alfred Hitchcock: Centenary Essays*, ed. Richard Allen and S. Ishii Gonzalès (London: BFI, 1999), 205-20; and Jack Sullivan, *Hitchcock's Music* (New Haven: Yale University Press, 2006). The first sentence in Sullivan's "Lethal Laughter" chapter is this: "For Hitchcock, comedy was essential" (183). For those interested in how Hitchcock's humor was incorporated into musical scores by his various composers, this is a must-read.

10. Wes D. Gehring, *Parody as Film Genre: "Never Give a Saga an Even Break"* (Westport, CT: Greenwood Publishing Group, 1999).

11. Thomas Schatz, "Hitchcock and the Studio System," *The Cambridge Companion to Alfred Hitchcock*, ed. Jonathan Freedman (New York: Cambridge University Press, 2015), 25-39.

12. For an ideological approach, see David R. Shumway, "Screwball Comedies: Constructing Romance, Mystifying Marriage," *Film Genre Reader* IV, ed. Barry Keith Grant (Austin: University of Texas Press, 2012), 463-83.

13. For a discussion of the reluctance among male critics to use the word rape in reference to *Blackmail*, see Tania Modleski, *The Women Who Knew Too Much*, 3rd ed. (New York: Routledge, 2016), 20, 128.

14. See Naremore, "Hitchcock and Humor," 25.

15. For a discussion of children in Hitchcock, see Lee Edelman, "Hitchcock's Future," in *Alfred Hitchcock: Centenary Essays*, 239-62, and Debbie Olson, *Children in the Films of Alfred Hitchcock* (New York: Palgrave/Macmillan, 2014).

16. R. Barton Palmer, "*Secret Agent*: Or, Coming in the from the Cold, Maugham Style," in *Hitchcock at the Source: The Auteur as*

Adaptor, ed. R. Barton Palmer and David Boyd (New York: SUNY Press, 2011), 89-101.

17. Noel King and Toby Miller, "*The Lady Vanishes* but She Won't Go Away," in *Hitchcock at the Source: The Auteur as Adaptor*, 102.

18. Dana Polan, "The Light Side of Genius: Hitchcock's *Mr. and Mrs. Smith* in the Screwball Tradition," in *Comedy/Cinema/Theory*, ed. Andrew Horton (Berkeley and Los Angeles: University of California Press, 1991), 151.

19. Smith, *Hitchcock: Suspense, Humour and Tone*, 49.

20. Janet Maslin, "Alfred Hitchcock," in *Alfred Hitchcock: Interviews*, ed. Sidney Gottlieb (Jackson, MS: University Press of Mississippi, 2003), 107.

21. Oriana Fallaci, "Alfred Hitchcock: Mr. Chastity," in *Alfred Hitchcock: Interviews*, 55.

22. William Paul, *Laughing/Screaming: Modern Hollywood Horror & Comedy* (New York: Columbia University Press, 1994), 410.

23. John Bruns, *Loopholes: Reading Comically*, with a new introduction (New York: Routledge, 2013).

24. François Truffaut, with Helen G. Scott, *Hitchcock*, rev. ed. (New York: Simon and Schuster, 1984), 347.

25. Bazin had already alluded to Hitchcock's cinema of disequilibrium as early as 1946, in his review of *Suspicion* (1941), which appeared in *L'Ecran français*, October 29, 1946: "Up until the final shot Hitchcock manages to make us walk a tightrope over an abyss, pushing us first lightly to the left, then to the right, catching us each time at the exact moment we think we're falling" (rpt. in *The Cinema of Cruelty*, 107).

26. Bazin, *The Cinema of Cruelty*, 154. See John Bruns, *Hitchcock's People, Places, and Things* (Evanston: Northwestern University Press, 2019), 89.

27. See Wes D. Gehring, *Carole Lombard: The Hoosier Tornado* (Indianapolis: Indiana Historical Society Press, 2003).

28. One might also include Jack and his partner Fred. But while they know Uncle Charlie is the suspected Merry Widow murderer, they too fail to fully grasp the danger Charlie is in. In fact, Jack is nowhere to be found the moment Charlie needs him most.

29. For a discussion of maternal desire—Emma's but also Jo McKenna's—see Elsie B. Michie's excellent essay, "Unveiling Maternal Desires: Hitchcock and American Domesticity," in *Hitchcock's America*, ed. Jonathan Freedman and Richard Milligan (New York: Oxford University Press, 1999), 29-54.

30. Hitchcock's attacks on marriage are so pervasive that Gehring suggests, in one of the book's many provocative passages, that *Rear Window*'s murder plot "is Hitchcock's MacGuffin," that it distracts from the film's true plot: marriage (197). This would be convincing were it not for the fact that in *Rear Window* (and, for that matter, *Shadow of a Doubt*, *Strangers on a Train*, and countless other Hitchcock films and television episodes) murder and marriage are inseparable.

DAVID STERRITT

The Guardians of Morality vs. the Master of Suspense

John Billheimer, *Hitchcock and the Censors*. Lexington: University Press of Kentucky, 2019. 370 pp. $50 cloth, $27.95 paperback.

Near the beginning of *Hitchcock and the Censors*, author John Billheimer describes the Motion Picture Production Code as "a self-inflicted wound that took over thirty-four years to heal, affecting more than eleven thousand films, weakening most and leaving only a few stronger for the encounter" (9). This is a ruefully accurate description as far as it goes, but as Billheimer demonstrates, Alfred Hitchcock had more than the Production Code Administration (PCA) dogging his cinematic trail over the course of his long career. In the early years, the British Board of Film Censors (BBFC) kept watch over his pictures. Starting in 1933, the Catholic Legion of Decency had a say when movies came to the American market, as did the PCA when it acquired its full clout in 1934. Other organizations also peered over Hitchcock's shoulder for all sorts of reasons: *Lifeboat* was vetted by the Office of War Information, the American Humane Association was very interested in *The Birds*, and the Department of the Interior had problems with plans for *North by Northwest*. Local and overseas censorship boards also stalked the earth, even though a major reason for instituting the Code was to put the inconsistent patchwork of regional snoopers out of business. Moviegoers in Maryland didn't see Bruno murder Miriam in *Strangers on a Train*; viewers in India didn't see Grace Kelly on James Stewart's lap in *Rear Window*; those watching *Lifeboat* in England saw the killing of Willi only in part; no one in Ireland saw *Notorious* at all. Such were the capricious penalties inflicted on dubious behavior in films by one of cinema's greatest artists. As a chronicle of misguided moralizing, Billheimer's volume makes for engrossing film-historical reading.

Led first by Will Hays and later by the more moderate Joseph Breen and Geoffrey Shurlock, watchdogs at the Code Office kept their eyes peeled mainly for sin, sex, violence, and crime, basing their judgments on a 4,000-word compendium of rules and guidelines. By contrast, their British counterparts started work in 1912 with only two strictures—no nudity, no depictions of Christ—and gradually expanded their mandate to cover everything from "indecorous dancing" to "relations between capital and labour" (36), with political matters getting the most emphasis. Billheimer's report on Hitchcock's interactions with the BBFC is unavoidably sketchy, since German planes bombed the agency's London office in 1941, destroying all firsthand records. It's nevertheless clear that the censors affected the director's work—vetoing his proposal for a hard-hitting film about the General Strike of 1926, for instance, and watering down his plan to reproduce the Siege of Sidney Street, a fabled gun battle of 1911, in the 1934 version of *The Man Who Knew Too Much*. "Again and again," he said in a 1938 magazine interview, "I have been prevented from putting on the screen authentic accounts of incidents in British life" (41). Yet he sometimes found it possible to outsmart BBFC chief Joseph Brooke Wilkinson, who ran the organization throughout the director's British years. In an irony worthy of a Hitchcock movie, England's most powerful film censor suffered from chronically declining eyesight. Sitting alongside him in the screening room, Hitchcock claimed later, he would say something to distract Wilkinson's attention, and if luck prevailed, "the scene went by . . . without his seeing it" (39).

Even as he outfoxed the BBFC, however, Hitchcock lost various battles with his own producers. He reluctantly acceded to front-office demands for relatively upbeat finales in *The Lodger: A Story of the London Fog* and *Blackmail*, and Gaumont British sliced more than five minutes from *The Man Who Knew Too Much* to appease American censors who saw "too much slaughter; too much gunplay; too much murdering of policemen" (44). Recognizing the PCA's growing strength, Gaumont sent the screenplay for *Secret Agent* to Hays and company before starting production, reckoning that the inevitable changes would be cheaper and easier on the page than in the editing room. Stumbling blocks in that film included the words "lover" and "connubial," as well as a sight gag involving the décolletage of young women. Also in question was the propriety of calling Peter Lorre's character "the hairless Mexican," which might offend Mexicans and people lacking hair; both the BBFC and the PCA wanted to avoid affronting foreign audiences, and while their battles over mild violence and sexual innuendo now seem quaint, their vigilance over ethnic and nationalistic slights is in tune with today's heightened sensitivity to such matters.

As things turned out, "the hairless Mexican" retained his moniker thanks to added dialogue specifying that he was not Mexican and had plenty of hair. But in *The Lady Vanishes* a toilet reference ("a private thingummy") did not make it to the screen—toilets were always troubling, and references in *Mr. and Mrs. Smith*, *The Paradine Case*, and *The Wrong Man* were all flushed down the drain—and the portion of *The 39 Steps* where Robert Donat and Madeleine Carroll are handcuffed to each other required much negotiation before it emerged (mostly) intact from BBFC vetting. Eager to please the American market for Hitchcock's last British thriller of the 1930s, coproducer Erich Pommer invited the PCA to meddle with *Jamaica Inn* at every stage, letting them dictate "the occupation of the villain, the level of violence in the pirate encounters, the incidence of profanity, and even the mind-set of the villain in his final scenes" (55). Hitchcock was eager for his impending move to Hollywood, but closer proximity to the Code Office was surely not one of the reasons.

After a brief overview of Hitchcock's vexed but productive partnership with producer extraordinaire David O. Selznick, the book details the censorship travails of *Rebecca*, their first joint venture. Selznick paid a hefty $50,000 for the rights to Daphne du Maurier's bestseller despite a PCA warning that emulating the novel's failure to punish Maxim de Winter, who has killed his wife, would be a "clear violation . . . since it apparently justifies and condones murder" (65). Breen and Shurlock reiterated their position over lunch with Hitchcock after receiving the script, whereupon Selznick's story editor, Val Lewton, started sending revisions to Breen every day, juggling these updates with Hitchcock's shooting schedule and a steady stream of Selznick's notoriously prolix memos.

Breen and his colleagues had three major demands: that murder not go unpunished, that the "quite inescapable inference of sex perversion" be expunged from Mrs. Danvers, and that dialogue not overemphasize the late Rebecca's extramarital love life. The filmmakers skirted the second and third of these reasonably well, but they caved on the issue of Maxim's unpunished murder, implementing Breen's idea that all difficulties would vanish if Rebecca's death resulted from an accident rather than a homicide. Hitchcock said he enjoyed his "spirited give and take" with Breen's office—it had "all the thrill of competitive horse trading," he told an interviewer (70)—and for Billheimer the *Rebecca* negotiation is one of many that prove the director's ability to strike effective bargains with the guardians of public propriety. Even so, Billheimer lists *Rebecca* as one of several instances where Hitchcock's low regard for story and subject—"You get your satisfaction through style of treatment. I'm not interested in content" (316)—resulted in regrettable compromises. Other examples are *Suspicion, I Confess, The Paradine Case,* and *Strangers on a Train*; since these all date from the 1940s and early 1950s, the implication is that Hitchcock got better at outsmarting and evading censorship in the later phases of his career.

Ideology could be as problematic as morality, especially in the tumultuous World War II era, and this partly shaped Hitchcock's second American picture, *Foreign Correspondent*, inspired by a war reporter's politically freighted memoir. If the film followed the source text too closely, the Code office fretted, it might "arouse audience feeling against the present German regime" (72). In addition to Hollywood's habitual nervousness about slighting foreigners and harming international ticket sales, studios now had to comply with the Neutrality Acts, instituted in the 1930s to constrain American involvement in entangling foreign affairs. No fewer than fourteen writers labored on the screenplay for *Foreign Correspondent*, which ultimately tossed out almost everything from the memoir, mentioned Adolf Hitler only once, and set its war in fictitious Borovia, a device that misled nobody into mistaking the identities of the story's obviously German villains. To cap the drama with a decisive message, Hitchcock recruited Ben Hecht to write a climactic radio speech for the war-reporter hero—"Hello America! Hang onto your lights! They are the only lights left in the world!"—with artful wording that could be construed as "pro-preparedness" rather than "anti-isolationist," thereby satisfying Neutrality Act requirements (76); with uncanny prescience, the peroration was filmed just five days before London suffered its first German bombing. During this period Hitchcock was deeply upset by some British cinema professionals who denounced him for cowering in Hollywood while others confronted the Nazis and endured the perils of war. Hitchcock was the opposite of a shirker, however, as Billheimer shows: he donated generous amounts of time, money, and energy to the war effort and finessed both the Code office and the Neutrality Acts to ensure the Allied bona fides of *Foreign Correspondent*. He also had the last laugh when *Foreign Correspondent* scored a critical and commercial success.

By the time *Lifeboat* went into production, Hitchcock had to contend with the government's recently formed Office of War Information (OWI) and its subsidiary Bureau of Motion

Pictures, basically a show-biz propaganda ministry. They found fault with almost every character in the screenplay: the executive was "unfairly unsympathetic," the engineer had a Communist tilt, the journalist was an "amoral . . . adventuress," and so on; worst of all, the Nazi they rescued had a more heroic temperament than any of them. Hitchcock could ignore the OWI, which had no enforcement power, and he successfully overlooked many of the Code office's complaints, although Twentieth Century Fox agreed to delete the broken-off phrase "son-of-a—" from all prints when it was noticed several weeks after release. Initial reviews were favorable, but the tide turned when *New York Times* critic Bosley Crowther took the OWI line, expressing his "sneaking suspicion that the Nazis, with some cutting here and there, could turn *Lifeboat* into a whiplash against the decadent democracies. And it is questionable whether such a picture . . . is judicious at this time" (104-07). Rattled by the controversy, studio chief Darryl F. Zanuck scuttled much of the film's advertising and promotion, sinking its earnings and putting a temporary dent in Hitchcock's rising American career.

The postwar years brought fresh rounds of censorial tampering, many of them well known to Hitchcock cognoscenti. Code officials signed off on the story of *Spellbound* but flagged numerous locutions in the screenplay, some inherent to the movie's psychoanalytical subject ("libido," "seduction complex"), others just generally objectionable ("playing tomcat," "Good Lord"). Breen also admonished Hitchcock to consult the BBFC, which always nixed movies about "lunatic asylums or insane people," and the FBI, since a key character was a federal agent (111). This was another Selznick project, and the producer balked at Hitchcock's insistence on hiring Salvador Dalí to design a bravura dream sequence, observing that religious groups regarded the great surrealist as a "very unsavory" figure (113). Dalí was hired but the dream sequence was reduced to a shadow of Hitchcock's grand conception, partly to cut costs and partly to avoid naughty Freudian symbols. Mixed reviews notwithstanding, the black-and-white melodrama stands as Selznick's most profitable release after the flamboyantly colorful *Gone with the Wind* (1939) and *Duel in the Sun* (1946). Not long thereafter, the romantic thriller *Notorious* stirred up preproduction trouble when Hitchcock and Hecht visited a leading physicist with what they thought was an innocent inquiry about the correct size of an atomic bomb, alarming the scientist—in the burgeoning cold war, some questions were no longer innocent—and prompting the FBI to surveil Hitchcock for several months. The biggest sex-related concern posed by *Notorious* involved the loose-living Ingrid Bergman character, and here Breen made the useful suggestion of changing her "from a woman who lived by her body to one who lived by her wits." This was a case where Code intervention actually improved a scenario, in Billheimer's well-reasoned opinion, since the alteration made the character more morally and psychologically complex. *Notorious* also occasioned what might be Hitchcock's most ingenious contravention of PCA prudery. Kisses couldn't last more than three seconds under an unofficial Code guideline, so Hitchcock cooked up the legendary scene where Bergman and Cary Grant embrace, nuzzle, nibble, and smooch for a nonstop two minutes and forty seconds, exchanging at least twenty kisses along the way, each clocking in below the three-second limit (125–26).

Rope, loosely inspired by the Leopold and Loeb murder case of 1924, has a surprisingly bold premise: two evidently gay men kill a friend to show their superiority over ordinary people, conceal the corpse in a trunk, and serve food to party guests (including the victim's father) from the de facto coffin. And the Code office had a surprisingly unperturbed reaction, finding little to criticize beyond drinking at the party and disrespect for the Ten Commandments in the dialogue. Since the picture's radically unusual style called for unedited takes up to ten minutes long, Hitchcock asked the Code office to review each reel when it was finished, and the picture emerged more or less as he envisioned it. What sailed past Breen didn't fare so well in the wider world, however. The president of Paramount wrote to the president of Warner

Bros. that the picture "too closely evoked the Leopold-Loeb case, with its portrait of two killers clearly homosexual and worse, Jewish" (146). It was banned in numerous American cities and several European countries, raising enough ruckus for the *New York Times* to declare that censorship was tying *Rope* in knots. Reasons for the restrictions varied: in Maryland and Ohio the main problem was the notion that committing murder could make a killer feel "exhilarated," whereas the Netherlands felt the film justified "elimination of persons of inferior intellect" (147). The filmmakers had veiled the gay subtext so deftly that few critics or censors seemed to notice it, much less be bothered by it, but the picture contained enough other provocations to strike many moralists as "not wholesome entertainment," in the Chicago police department's words. Hitchcock's next film was the Bergman vehicle *Under Capricorn*, and here Breen was less exercised by the morality of the movie than by the wounded reputation of its star, whose marriage-ending affair with Italian filmmaker Roberto Rossellini was making headlines. Breen wrote to her personally, begging her to "deny the rumors" and reassure her fans, which she couldn't do because the rumors were true. Catholic groups and theater owners condemned the film and a United States Senator deplored Bergman as an "apostle of degradation" on the Capitol floor. Hurt by the morality attacks, the movie's cinematic flaws, or both, *Under Capricorn* failed at the box office and joined with *Rope* in putting a premature end to Hitchcock's newly formed production company.

Cracks appeared in the Production Code as the 1950s progressed, but caveats, cautions, and demands continued to appear. To receive approval for *Strangers on a Train*, the filmmakers altered the breakup of Guy's marriage, putting the onus on the wife rather the "sympathetic lead," and amended Bruno's ruminations about homicide, deleting his opinion that murder is "not against the law of nature" (170-01). Hitchcock hired a Roman Catholic theologian to assure the technical and ethical correctness of *I Confess*, but that churchy drama nevertheless drew more suggestions from the

Code office than any of the director's other films, many of them concerning details that "no non-Catholic and relatively few Catholics would have recognized . . . as gaffes" (181). In a clever diplomatic move, Hitchcock invited Code representatives to the set of *Rear Window* so they could see with their own eyes how safely distant some of the story's spicier details—honeymooners enjoying each other's company, Miss Torso in her skimpy togs—would be when viewed by audiences. The maneuver worked so well that the picture's heavy reliance on voyeurism also escaped censure, even though voyeurism had been a hot-button topic for the Code since its inception. Hitchcock preserved the sexy essence of the fireworks scene in *To Catch a Thief* by toning down the music score and trading away a mild sight gag and a bit of dialogue elsewhere in the film. One of the few thorny points in *Vertigo* lay in the law's failure to punish Gavin Elster for engineering his wife's murder, which Hitchcock solved with a tacked-on radio broadcast announcing Elster's arrest; this coda was deleted when the film went into release, although censors retained it in some foreign markets. Worries about *North by Northwest* included Leonard's subtly suggested homosexuality and dialogue about Thornhill's serial marriages, and Hitchcock handled them with ease, although he complied with a request that Cary Grant and Eva Marie Saint maintain an angle of forty-five degrees between their embracing bodies and the mattress of their sleeping-car berth. Greater effort was needed to overcome United Nations officials' refusal of permission to film in the UN building or on its grounds, and the Department of the Interior put a similar kibosh on shooting at the Mount Rushmore National Monument; even when Hitchcock replaced Mount Rushmore with a large-scale studio model, authorities limited the bits and pieces of statuary that could appear on the screen.

At the start of the 1960s, the Code was unmistakably showing its age, and Hitchcock took advantage of its declining sway as Hollywood moved toward replacing the PCA with the MPAA rating system, which debuted in 1968. Not surprisingly, Code officials had numerous objections to the script for *Psycho*, from the flushing toilet to the suggestion of incest between Norman and his mother before her death, but Hitchcock had a list of items he was fully prepared to sacrifice for the sake of retaining the elements that mattered most to him. The shower scene posed particular challenges for the censors: in one screening, three reviewers detected nudity and two did not; in a second screening of the same print, the first three did not see it but the other two now did. Surely much amused, Hitchcock deleted a single shot (showing Marion's bare buttocks) and thereby saved the scene. *The Birds* was affected less by the Code than by the Humane Association, which rode herd over the production and furiously objected to a climactic scene of mass devastation—"It looked like Armageddon," the storyboard artist said—that Hitchcock ultimately decided not to shoot, substituting the famously unresolved conclusion that he preferred. The most predictable problem with *Marnie* was the scene of marital rape, but its allusive, inexplicit imagery breezed past the censors without delay. By the time of *Topaz*, the Code was as dead as Mrs. Bates, and Hitchcock prepared to shoot the key sex scene with more visible flesh than ever before, only to discover that the bodies of both actors, Karin Dor and Frederick Stafford, were marked by surgical scars. "Very well, then. We shall film the scene from the shoulders up," ordered the disappointed but ever-resilient director (300).

Frenzy found Hitchcock ready to present violence and nudity with newfound freedom, jolting the screen with a scene of rape and murder more savage than anything else in his filmography. It would have been even more savage if Hitchcock had included a close-up of blood and saliva coming from the victim's mouth, but screenwriter Anthony Shaffer warned that moviegoers would find this "disgusting," and the director deleted it from the final cut. But he included it in the version sent to the British censors, who were still in business; they demanded a little trimming in the rape scene and passed everything else in the picture. Hitchcock's only subsequent film, *Family Plot*, is so tame that nearly all of it would have passed muster had the Code still been operative.

An account of this mild dramedy gives Billheimer's book a similarly mild final chapter, followed by a brief concluding portion that reemphasizes Hitchcock's brilliance as a bargainer, his belief in the priority of images over words, and the extent to which Code requirements arguably improved a handful of films.

Billheimer is primarily a mystery writer, which may explain why *Hitchcock and the Censors* shows more interest in spinning anecdotes than in theorizing about the sociocultural issues they raise. Asked in 1938 why his films generally shied away from public affairs, for instance, Hitchcock cited censorship pressures, saying that "circumstances have forced me into the realm of fiction. I have always wanted to make films with some sociological importance—but I have never been allowed to do so" (40). This would have been a fascinating area for Billheimer to explore, but he allows it to pass with little comment. As to his writing, the book is always clear and very regular in its structure, with most chapters giving plot synopses, descriptions of production circumstances, discussions of censorship matters, and summaries of critical and box-office responses. Flaws of the study include minor errors, as when Dr. Edwardes becomes Dr. Edwards in the discussion of *Spellbound*, and repetition, as when the climax of *Jamaica Inn* is twice described in near-identical language. Although it is not a probing book, Hitchcock aficionados will find much pleasure in *Hitchcock and the Censors*, which provides abundant evidence of how far mainstream cinema has traveled—for better and perhaps for worse—from its earlier history in more straitlaced, censorious times.

Henry K. Miller

Hitchcock's Spy Films

James Chapman, *Hitchcock and the Spy Film*. London: I.B. Tauris, 2018. 360 pp. $36 cloth.

In "Hitchcock's Vision," one of his most penetrating essays, uncollected to this day, Peter Wollen compared Hitchcock with "perhaps the major influence on his work," John Buchan.[1] "For Buchan," wrote Wollen, "the game of adventure, the pursuit, the combat, had a purpose, ultimately a political purpose, the defence of an empire and a way of life." The essay begins with a quotation from Buchan's 1913 serial *The Power-House*—published as a book in 1916 after the success of the previous year's *The Thirty-Nine Steps*: "Now I saw how thin is the protection of civilization . . . ." For Hitchcock, however, "this purpose has evaporated. The struggle takes place over a MacGuffin, a mere pretext which in its perfect form, as Hitchcock repeatedly emphasizes, is simply nothing, a void." Rather, espionage took on psychological significance, above all as a pretext for staging voyeurism. The Imperial connection is not incidental: one of Hitchcock's fullest discussions of the MacGuffin, in Truffaut's interview book, traced its roots to the stories of a writer who is practically synonymous with Imperialism, Kipling. "Many of them were spy stories, and they were concerned with the efforts to steal the secret plans out of a fortress. The theft of secret documents was the original MacGuffin."[2] These documents mattered to the characters, who were trying to preserve the security of the Raj, but to Hitchcock "they're of no importance whatever."

James Chapman's *Hitchcock and the Spy Film* sets out to "locate his spy films in their wider cultural and institutional contexts" (1), arguing that hitherto Hitchcock has been largely the province of auteurists who see Hitchcock's films as Hitchcock films rather than genre films, disregarding the seedbed of espionage fiction, both literary and cinematic, from which they flowered, and ignoring the industrial conditions in which they were made, above all by eliding the difference between British and American systems. There is a chapter on each of the spy films—*The Man Who Knew Too Much*, *The 39 Steps*, *Secret Agent*, *Sabotage*, *The Lady Vanishes*, *Foreign Correspondent*, *Saboteur*, *Notorious*, *The Man Who Knew Too Much* again, *North By Northwest*, *Torn Curtain*, and *Topaz*—plus chapters on "Hitchcock and British Cinema" and "Hitchcock and American Cinema," as well as one on Hitchcock and James Bond. In Chapman's view, it was with Hitchcock's 1930s thrillers "that the spy film really emerged as a genre in its own right" (8), and in his introduction, "Authorship, Genre, National Cinema," he gives a brief overview of the genre's largely British ancestry, distinguishing between two schools of spy fiction, the sensational and the realist. Buchan, "Sapper" (creator of Bulldog Drummond), and Ian Fleming belong to the first school; Joseph Conrad, Somerset Maugham, Eric Ambler, and John le Carré to the second. Hitchcock, says Chapman, straddled the two sub-genres.

The identity of the auteurists whom Chapman frequently invokes is a matter for conjecture; except for the original *Cahiers du cinéma* critics of the 1950s and their Anglo-American followers of the 1960s, none are named. It is hard to think of anyone now writing for whom "everything in the film is seen as the outcome of the director's creative agency and as an expression of his 'worldview'" (4). If it is the case that the auteurist "emphasis on the individuality and uniqueness of the *auteur* neglects any comparative framework that considers what their films might have in common with, as well as how they are different from, those of other filmmakers working in the same institutional and cultural contexts" (4), then Rohmer and Chabrol were not auteurists; they are quoted as calling *The 39 Steps* "a perfect example of the thriller in its pure state—so much so that it has as an essential characteristic the essence of every thriller" (55), a judgment that suggests some awareness of genre. Nor would it have been news to them that there were differences between Hitchcock's British and American films; they actually distinguished between films made in different British studios. In practice, the nameless "auteurists" are an Aunt Sally conjured up to make Chapman's discussion of Hitchcock's place in the spy genre, and his place in the two major industries in which he worked, seem more against-the-grain than it really is.

Still, it is probably true that the British films suffer from neglect, and Chapman is right to argue that they "established many of the characteristic 'Hitchcockian' motifs that were to recur throughout his work" (15)—a judgment that was obvious to Hitchcock's contemporaries, but has been somewhat drowned out since in the din of commentary. Whereas the production histories of the American films are well-covered in other books, the industrial context for the British films which made Hitchcock's name internationally is less familiar territory, and there is consequently more potential for fresh insights. Paradoxically, however, the besetting problem here is Chapman's insistence on seeing the British films as belonging to an industrial context distinct from the American; on one page he refers to "fully British films" and "British films per se" (127), but it is arguable that none of the films under discussion should be so described. "There was a quite remarkable stability in key production personnel throughout the 'classic thriller sextet'" (20), he writes, and this was provided by the Gaumont-British Picture Corporation, which was founded in 1927 and began to founder about a decade later. In fact, the fifth of the six, *Young and Innocent*, from 1937, was made in quite different circumstances from the first four, and the sixth, *The Lady Vanishes*, from 1938, in even more different circumstances, so it was more of a remarkably stable quartet; nevertheless, an account of Gaumont-British is essential to an understanding of the sextet's production, and a salient question is how "fully British" it was.

By the time Hitchcock joined Gaumont-British in 1934, the controlling stake in the corporation was held by the Ostrer brothers, merchant bankers who had bought out the French interest in the company some ten years earlier. Until recently they had held 49% of the stock, but around 1932 they had taken that to 51%. The other 49% of Gaumont-British—or rather the Metropolis and Bradford Trust which controlled it—was held by Fox, whose president Sidney Kent sat on the Gaumont-British board. This is not arcane information, but it is surprising how little it figures in accounts of British cinema—including Chapman's book, which simply does not mention it. Forty-nine percent may be the minority stake, but any account of "industrial and economic conditions" (4), especially one that makes such a show of attacking the auteurists who ignore them, would surely have to at least mention this connection with one of the Hollywood majors. It matters especially when Chapman discusses the fate of Hitchcock's British films in the U.S., since it would be interesting to know if the Fox tie-up made a difference. But again, Chapman's interest in the films' industrial context does not extend much beyond the home market, and there are only vague references to their distribution in the America. A claim that "The appeal of the Hitchcock films in the United States seems to have been primarily for cineastes in larger metropolitan centres" (23) is supported solely by an undated press clipping from a file about *The Lady Vanishes* in the Academy of Motion Picture Arts and Sciences (AMPAS) collection.

The Man Who Knew Too Much, it is claimed, "had a limited release in America: it seems to have done well at metropolitan cinemas specializing in foreign films such as the Belasco in Washington, DC, and the Mayfair in New York (where it was held over for three weeks)" (47), while "Like *The Man Who Knew Too Much*, *The 39 Steps* was most successful in the larger metropolitan centres" (67). Since the establishment of the Media History Digital Library, there does not need to be so much "seems to" about these estimates. *Variety* covered the Gaumont-British films' U.S. distribution well enough to make more definite judgments possible, and most of these claims are simply wrong. *The Man Who Knew Too Much* played all over. The Mayfair was a Times Square theater that had gone over to films, with no discernible bias towards the foreign; *The Man Who Knew Too Much* replaced *Times Square Lady* and was replaced by a Philo Vance mystery, *The Casino Murder Case*, both MGM productions. The trade papers focused on first-run city cinemas, so it is more difficult to know how the films fared elsewhere, but given Chapman's refusal to provide evidence to back up his assertions, his implied claims about the films' lack of appeal in the sticks must be treated with extreme caution. Even if Hitchcock's films did play better in "metropolitan centres"—meaning cities like St. Louis, Pittsburgh, and Buffalo—it is not obvious why "cineastes" should be invoked.

By the time of *The Lady Vanishes*, Gaumont-British had gone through a great crisis, and so it was, as Chapman writes, "the first film under a new distribution agreement between Gaumont-British and MGM, whereby the latter would act as distributor for the studio's films at home and abroad" (110). MGM did indeed distribute *The Lady Vanishes* in Britain, but not in the U.S., where *Variety* gives variations on "20th," "20th-Fox-GB," "20th-GB," and "GB" as the distributor.[3] According to Chapman, "the MGM deal was seen at the time as evidence of the growing interest in British films in America; on the other hand, it was also a symptom of Gaumont-British's failure to establish its own distribution network in the United States" (110). No evidence is given for the first of these claims, and the second just seems to be an invention. It is not that Gaumont-British was a towering success stateside—clearly something went wrong—rather that Chapman is not a reliable judge of its fortunes. For a film made in a tiny studio with no American stars, *The Lady Vanishes* did quite well in the U.S. It would be interesting to know if either Fox or MGM or both put up an advance to get it made, but we do not learn anything about this; the idea is not entertained. The real industrial context for Hitchcock's "British" films of the 1930s remains a subject for further research.

Chapman's treatment of genre is similarly frustrating, because Hitchcock's "literary" hinterland is another under-explored field—literary in quote-marks because not all of it meets the distinct meaning commonly given to "literature" or "literary fiction." Chapman's basic taxonomy of spy fiction into realist and sensational schools is unobjectionable, but is never developed much beyond this point, and a reading of the genre's politics is barely attempted. When he quotes Hitchcock's "no importance whatever" (4) definition of the MacGuffin, for example, the references to Kipling are concealed by ellipses. By coincidence, he quotes exactly the same passage from *The Power-House* as Wollen (9-10), but gives no consideration to what "civilization" meant to Buchan in 1913—or to Hitchcock, later on. When Chapman compares Buchan's *The Thirty-Nine Steps* with Hitchcock's *The 39 Steps*, he writes that "the abstract 'MacGuffin' that sets the plot in motion" (55) was there in the original, intending to show that the film followed the book more closely than is sometimes supposed; but he misses Wollen's point that the MacGuffin in Hitchcock really is abstract, whereas in Buchan (and Kipling) it is not. One may well concur that "the key moments in the development of spy fiction have been during periods of ideological tension in global politics" (6), but which periods, during Hitchcock's life, or, indeed, before and after it, would that exclude?

The treatment of writers Hitchcock is fairly likely to have read in his formative years is superficial. There are fleeting references to the leading mystery novelists of the pre-Buchan period, William Le Queux and E. Phillips Oppenheim, "with their tales of intrigue in the courts and governments of Europe" (7), or alternatively "tales of intrigue and conspiracy in the courts and governments of Continental Europe" (50), but one could stand to know more about these writers than these two clauses provide. In a review of an important book on genre fiction, Richard Usborne's *Clubland Heroes*, first published in 1953, the British novelist Julian Maclaren-Ross wrote that until the publication of *The Thirty-Nine Steps*, Le Queux and Oppenheim

> had this literary field more or less to themselves; theirs was a less realistic convention, stiff and formalised in manner: the crackle of starched shirts could be heard between the sentences as suave diplomats skirmished with barbed politeness over dinner-tables in cosmopolitan restaurants or in "the chancelleries of Europe." Buchan's swifter pace and colloquial style, containing homely echoes of *King Solomon's Mines* and *Allan Quartermain*, was to alter all that.[4]

In a separate essay from 1955, "Out of the Ordinary: The Novel of Pursuit and Suspense," likewise touching on Buchan's antecedents, Maclaren-Ross wrote that Buchan had "adapted the sense of helpless terror conveyed in the first part of *Treasure Island* to a metropolitan setting and surroundings even more prosaic than those described in *The Suicide Club* or *The Rajah's Diamond*."[5] Chapman does not quote or cite either of these essays, but writes that Buchan "represented a shift away from the cloak-and-dagger world of the Oppenheim-Le Queux tradition: instead its fast-paced narrative of action and pursuit drew upon the conventions of late nineteenth-century imperial adventure fiction such as Robert Louis Stevenson and H. Rider Haggard" (50), the former being the author of *Treasure Island*, *The Suicide Club*, and *The Rajah's Diamond*; the latter being the author of *King Solomon's Mines* and *Allan Quartermain*. These are avenues of research to be pursued, not repeated. In his study of crime fiction, *Snobbery with Violence*, first published in 1971, Colin Watson devoted a chapter to Le Queux and Oppenheim that emphasizes their fondness for the casino world of the French Riviera—as well as the chancelleries of Europe—irresistibly suggesting a connection with *To Catch a Thief*.[6]

Chapman repeatedly makes declarations along the lines of "*Saboteur* was also the product of a different set of historical and ideological contexts than *The 39 Steps*" (168), but never addresses the question whether the difference between the two civilizations that needed to be protected in the British and American films—the difference between the declining British Empire and ascendant American one—was of much significance to Hitchcock. Chapman's unstated assumption is rather that the same civilization was at stake in the struggle against Nazism and Communism, which are the main "historical contexts" on display. That the two films are so similar, and that the pronounced difference between British and American civilizations seems to have been so negligible to Hitchcock, rather supports Wollen's point that the struggle in his films was over a void, without political purpose. Chapman, however, is intent on arguing that the films are meaningfully political. One of his claims is the idea that *Sabotage* reflected "contemporary anxieties around subversion and political terrorism" (96), evidenced with a reference to IRA atrocities three years after its release; but usually it means little more than pointing out that the bad guys in the British films could plausibly be seen as German, or, in the case of the remake of *The Man Who Knew Too Much*, "implicitly East European" (208). There is ultimately no pretense that the films try to grapple with ideological questions, however; as Chapman himself says of *Notorious*, "the Nazi conspirators could have been changed to Communists without making any real difference" (190).

The insistence, despite this admission, that all of Hitchcock's spy films had significant political content, were "a vehicle for exploring the ideological tensions of the time" (29), and that some of them could be described as "realist," flattens out the difference between the overwhelming majority of them and the only one with pretensions to realism, *Topaz*, the last of them. While the division into realist and sensational is broadly unobjectionable for the spy genre in general, and while it has some bearing on Hitchcock's films, it is not a framework of such compelling value that it needs to be applied where it doesn't fit, and that is surely the case with *Notorious*, which Chapman somehow finds himself describing as "squarely within the realist-existential lineage of the spy thriller" (178).

More generally speaking, Chapman has a weakness for coat-trailing arguments that on more than one occasion end up contradicting themselves. He calls *Spellbound* "Hitchcock's first American film with top-rank stars" (175), then goes on to say that at Warners Hitchcock was obliged to work with "lesser stars"; even Montgomery Clift "did not have the same marquee value as Cary Grant" (195)—who had, of course, acted for Hitchcock before *Spellbound*, as had Carole Lombard. Besides which, it was on another of the Warners films that Hitchcock worked with Marlene Dietrich. Elsewhere, Chapman writes that "Hitchcock was not regarded primarily as a thriller director before making *The Man Who Knew Too Much*" (15-16), and that he was more often associated with "the theatrical or literary adaptation," presumably because these outnumbered thrillers among the pre-1934 films. No references are given for this novel but not completely implausible claim, but though he does not remark upon it, Chapman's own citations of contemporary reviews for the Gaumont-British *Man Who Knew Too Much* make clear that Hitchcock was seen as a thriller director who had gone astray, and that the new film marked a "return to form" (45). Later, he writes that "*Rebecca* was an unusual film for Hitchcock in that it was not a suspense thriller but rather a romantic novel" (131), in which case wouldn't it actually mark a return to what he was best known for?

More seriously, this is a revealing assessment of *Rebecca*'s place in the Hitchcock canon. If *Notorious* is neither a sensational nor a realist thriller, it may more usefully be seen as belonging to a central tendency in Hitchcock's films, along with *Rebecca*: they are both "women's pictures" that turn on the problem of subjectivity. Among the spy films, *The Lady Vanishes* and to a lesser extent *Sabotage* belong to it too. This is not to say that these are simply Hitchcock films rather than genre films—God forbid—but "genre" is a moveable feast, and it is worth noting that none of Chapman's archival findings demonstrate that Hitchcock or his producers thought of "the spy film" as a definite, confining set of attributes. *The Lodger*, the novel on which "first true Hitchcock" was based, is told strictly from the point of view of a female protagonist, and most of his films were based on or inspired by other texts, and rode the currents of cinematic fashion, and so on and so forth; in this sense they were genre films. But they are of interest outside of their "cultural and institutional contexts" in large part because Hitchcock directed them with distinction; that is all that the auteurist perspective amounts to, and while it's of limited—but not negligible—use as history, it's an acceptable starting-point for criticism.

The useful or original parts of Chapman's book are his discoveries in the archives of the British censorship board, which cast light on the films' development, revealing— more or less against Chapman's thesis—that even had Hitchcock wanted to explore "ideological tensions" in his films, the censor wouldn't have passed it. The AMPAS archives have been more extensively mined, but Chapman's gleanings about the writing of the second *Man Who Knew Too Much* in particular are valuable, showing that Angus MacPhail deserves more credit than he has been given; these however make up a small proportion of the whole, and more could be said, for example, about Hitchcock's crediting MacPhail with the invention of the MacGuffin, or about MacPhail's friendship with another Hitchcock collaborator, Ivor Montagu, who was at one time a Soviet asset if not actually a spy.

Notes

1. Peter Wollen, "Hitchcock's Vision," *Cinema* (Cambridge, England), no. 3 (June 1969): 2-4.

2. François Truffaut, with the collaboration of Helen G. Scott, *Hitchcock,* rev. ed. (New York: Simon & Schuster, 1984), 138.

3. See respectively *Variety*, 21 December 1938, 9; 11 January 1939, 9; 22 February 1939, 7; and 26 April 1939, 10.

4. Julian Maclaren-Ross, "A Totem of the 1920s," in *Bitten by the Tarantula and Other Writing* (London: Black Spring Press, 2005), 347.

5. Maclaren-Ross, "Out of the Ordinary: The Novel of Pursuit and Suspense," in *Bitten by the Tarantula*, 351.

6. Colin Watson, *Snobbery with Violence* (London: Faber and Faber, 2009).

NATHALIE MORRIS

The Forgotten Woman Behind Hitchcock

Christina Lane, *Phantom Lady: Hollywood Producer Joan Harrison, The Forgotten Woman Behind Hitchcock*. Chicago: Chicago Review Press, 2020. 400 pp. $30 cloth.

A "golden-haired ball of fire" is how legendary Hollywood columnist Hedda Hopper described Joan Harrison in 1945. By then, Harrison had three films under her belt as a producer, as well as multiple screenwriting credits and the distinction of being the first screenwriter to have two Oscar nominations in the same year (for *Rebecca* and *Foreign Correspondent*). Harrison's first film as producer, *Phantom Lady* (1944), set the tone for her subsequent films, which, as Christina Lane argues in this compelling and richly-researched biography, present "female-centric investigative thrillers" (5), and make a firm case for Harrison as a "producer-auteur" (6).

Harrison was also an astute self-publicist. She and her films frequently made column inches in 1940s Hollywood. The press loved to report on the phenomenon of a glamorous female producer "with dimples and a twenty-four-inch waist." Harrison cultivated and exploited this image, recognizing the importance of self-promotion to build her brand and gain power within the studio system. She had, of course, learned this from a master of the art, having spent nearly a decade of working with Alfred Hitchcock, first as secretary-assistant and then as a valued screenwriter.

Phantom Lady opens with Harrison's job interview with Hitchcock in 1933. Responding to a newspaper advert requesting a "young lady . . . for producer of films,"

Harrison cut short breakfast in bed and hightailed it from her upper middle class parents' home in Surrey to Lime Grove Studios in London. Pretending her sister was in labor, and that she needed to get back to the hospital, she managed to get bumped up in the queue and seen before the position was filled. Attracted by both Harrison's good looks and her macabre interest in true crime (her uncle was in charge of assigning cases at the Old Bailey), Hitchcock offered her the job. Whereas a lack of interest in being a secretary—soon to be apparent—could have meant a short tenure for Harrison, Hitchcock, as Lane observes, recognized her keen sense of story and brought her into the fold as a protégé and sounding board, soon to become a constant third point of "the triangular pattern that structured Hitchcock's creativity" (47).

This triangle was usually formed by Hitchcock, his wife Alma Reville, and a third writer, or number of writers (in the 1930s, this third writer was more often than not Charles Bennett). Lane explores the complexities of the dynamic brought about by Harrison's arrival, noting the way her creative role overlapped with, and even usurped, Reville's, as well as Hitchcock's clear and ongoing infatuation with the blonde Harrison. Speculation on Harrison's rise, and her relationship with Hitchcock, remained ongoing questions into the 1940s and beyond, with Harrison's eventual successor, Peggy Robertson, asking Hitchcock if he and Harrison had ever slept together. She felt that his reply—"I can say with complete conviction that I was never between the sheets with Joan"—was dissembling. "'Well that's not saying much,' retorted Robertson. 'What about on the hearth-rug, in the haystack, over the kitchen table?' Hitch gave a convincing look of horror. 'Do people really do things like that?'"(107).

Lane's conclusion is that Hitchcock's infatuation with Harrison, as with so many others, was from afar, although not necessarily benign. She touches on his problematic relationship with women through an anecdote from early in his association with Harrison, when he attempted to embarrass her by reading from the toilet scene in James Joyce's *Ulysses*. Harrison rose to the bait and lost her composure, apparently the only time she let the director get the better of her. Lane situates this within some of Hitchcock's public comments on women around this time, citing an article in *Film Weekly* that is revealing of his insecurities around class as well as his appeal—or lack of—to women. (Harrison could have initially aroused these anxieties in Hitchcock on both counts.) While Lane observes that Hitchcock's comments were often tongue-in-cheek, she notes that he could also be "caustic" and "chilling" (42).

But of course, Hitchcock's relationships with, and towards, women were not uncomplicated. His longstanding personal and creative partnership with Reville, as well as Harrison and later Peggy Robertson (and shorter-term writers such as Jay Presson Allen), demonstrate the value he placed on his female collaborators. He was, as Lane argues, "a bona fide teacher [with] a zeal for mentoring women" (46). Reville, of course, did not require this mentoring—Hitchcock learnt from her— but Harrison had an innate sense of story (and love of the macabre) that resonated with Hitchcock and encouraged him to invest in her training. Harrison learnt from Reville, too, and was soon indispensable to the couple's creative process. She spent Christmases with them in St. Moritz, contributing to script development and learning their system of crafting a film. By 1937, at a time when the Hitchcocks were exploring a move to Hollywood, Harrison had become so essential that the director insisted she be part of any deal. She not only understood what Lane describes as the Hitchcocks' "private code," "a specific language that Hitchcock had developed in concert with Alma, which translated the screenplay into a blueprint for production" (74), she had also proven herself as a force more important than any single screenwriter. She was "essentially performing the role of a creative producer," providing "vision of continuity and voice, especially when the revision process was rigorous" (74). This role, and her firm understanding of the Hitchcock brand, were exactly what made Harrison so indispensable to Hitchcock nearly two decades later when she took the helm of *Alfred Hitchcock Presents* (1955-62) and *The Alfred Hitchcock Hour* (1962-65).

Lane argues that one of Harrison's driving motivations was the desire to present the woman's angle, with a particular interest in female-centric crime stories in which women take on an active, investigative role. She traces the first evidence of this back to *Young and Innocent* (1937), the first film on which Harrison had significant input. Harrison had read Josephine Tey's *A Shilling for Candles* and proposed it to Hitchcock in 1936. Lane suggests that "it made perfect sense that the first film on which Joan began to have major input was jump-started by a female twist [making Nova Pilbeam's character the main character]." She notes that "it usher[ed] in the beginning of an era dominated by female-generated source material and women's genres, an earmark of the sensibilities that would be associated with Hitchcock for the foreseeable future" (65).

Harrison was instrumental in pushing for and securing Daphne du Maurier's *Rebecca* as Hitchcock's first Hollywood project, and was heavily involved in scripting, casting, and arguing (largely unsuccessfully) that the unnamed heroine become more assertive. For Hitchcock's next project, *Foreign Correspondent* (1940), Lane argues that the complex and intelligent Carol was "Joan's handiwork, early traces of an imprint that would soon show itself more forcibly" (105). *Suspicion* (1941) was another story of suspense and female investigation, largely written by Harrison and Reville before Samuel Raphaelson was brought on board to fine tune. Despite the problems over its ending (how could Cary Grant be a murderer?), the film was well-received and represented Harrison's and Reville's closest collaboration. Lane celebrates their working relationship, wondering "did the pair of women recognize the irony that they were collaborating—and apparently without much friction—on the story of a suspicious wife contemplating . . . the ambivalent, fatal places a marriage can go?' (123).

Alma Reville emerges from this biography as elusive and inscrutable as ever. She told reporters that working with

Harrison on *Suspicion* occasioned arguments "of course. But no bad feeling. I'd just as soon work with a woman as a man, just so long as she's good" (118). As Lane notes, by the time of *Foreign Correspondent*, Harrison was on an equal footing with Reville in terms of her involvement in the creative process, and onlookers wondered about the dynamics of the trio. On evenings out, Hitchcock would often "stand close to Joan as if he were escorting a movie star, shunting his wife to the margins." At dinners, Harrison was frequently seated next to Hitchcock, with Reville on her other side, and Lane highlights the frequency of this choreography in photographs of Harrison and the Hitchcocks from the time (107).

One of the many strengths of the book is the depth of its archival research and the use of the original interviews that Lane conducted with Harrison and the Hitchcocks' friends and colleagues and their children. Norman Lloyd, who worked with and observed them over many years, suggested that Reville knew exactly what she was doing: "If it ever appeared that Joan and Hitchcock were closer than they should have been, such as at public events, you have to realize that was Alma's staging" (108). It has been observed, in both scholarly studies and fictionalized portrayals of the couple, that Reville allowed room for her husband's fantasy life in order to facilitate his creative imagination. In some instances, his longings overstepped the mark, as in the case of Tippi Hedren. But with Joan Harrison, these yearnings underpinned a fertile period of his career, a contention Lane supports: "Alma seemingly allowed a certain amount of room for the mentoring relationship between and Joan and Hitch to play out so as to give Hitchcock's desires free rein inside his head" (108).

But Harrison did not want to always be contained within the world of Hitchcock and his films, and would soon prove herself as a dynamic, determined, and creative force in her own right. She left, with his reluctant blessing, during the making of *Saboteur* (1942), to strike out on her own as a screenwriter. Lane charts Harrison's early experiences with projects that went nowhere, such as *Hong Kong*, a proposed

Charles Boyer vehicle, and *The Sun is My Undoing*, which was to star Clark Gable. Lane notes that their failure to get made, after the departure of their star names, was a shock after Harrison's long stint working with such an established director. After two further disappointments (*First Comes Courage* [1943], on which director Dorothy Arzner was replaced by Charles Vidor, and *The Seventh Cross* [1944], where she was uncredited), she wanted to work on a project she felt passionately about. She secured the rights for Cornell Woolrich's *Phantom Lady* and began to develop a script. Turned down by several studios, she eventually took it to Universal, who offered her a contract to rewrite the script to their specifications. When she refused, they made the surprising suggestion that she instead produce the film herself.

With this move, Harrison became the only woman producer at a major Hollywood studio. *Phantom Lady* was a success, kickstarting Universal's production of both quality films and *films noir*. With *Phantom Lady*, Harrison demonstrated her interest in female-centric narratives and showed that she was a talented and capable producer. She made interesting casting choices, using Franchot Tone against type and finding a new star in Ella Raines, and the success of *Phantom Lady* opened the door for other women producers such as Virginia Van Upp at Columbia and Harriet Parsons at RKO. (Highlighting their solidarity, Lane notes that the women were spotted huddled together at cocktail parties, talking business). Lane's account of the production of *Phantom Lady* and her analysis of the film itself are illuminating, describing it as a "feminist odyssey" that inhabits women's spaces, utilizes fashion in its storytelling, and was designed to appeal to an audience of post-war working women (153). It also, notably, undermines the expectation of the titular "phantom lady" being a dark and destructive alter ego of the film's heroine, Carol (Ella Raines).

Phantom Lady paved the way for other successful projects such as *Dark Waters* (1944), an atmospheric gothic thriller with Merle Oberon; *Nocturne* (1946), a *noir* murder-mystery set in Hollywood, and *They Won't Believe Me* (1947), a film that plays with an unreliable narrator and features a shocking denouement. After quitting RKO with the arrival of Howard Hughes (who declared that all films would from thereon be about "fighting or fornication"), and observing the rise of the anti-Communist House Un-American Activities Committee (HUAC), Harrison began to question her place within late-1940s Hollywood. After a short but successful partnership with actor-turned-producer-director Robert Montgomery, which included the striking *Ride the Pink Horse* (1947), she embarked on a pair of U.K.-U.S. co-productions in England before realizing that her film work had dried up. But, Harrison's subsequent move into television, rather than marking the end of her career, began one of her most satisfying creative periods, as producer of *Alfred Hitchcock Presents* and *The Alfred Hitchcock Hour*.

Harrison had come full-circle. Everything she had learnt about the Hitchcock brand came together to "create the sense that Hitchcock's films and his television series—despite the fact in the series' ten year run he had only directed 18 out of 359 episodes—had an almost seamless relationship" (261). Lane points out that it was super-agent and head of MCA, Lew Wasserman, who initially suggested that Harrison had the perfect mix of talents to run the show, enabling Hitchcock to take only minimal involvement once he and Harrison had established the direction and tone of the series. Harrison had overall responsibility for almost everything, from selecting material and clearing rights to overseeing casting, selecting personnel and keeping sponsors happy, all the while keeping to tight deadlines. "It takes all the running you can do to stay in one place," she wrote in a guest column in the *LA Times*. Harrison also directly oversaw production of Hitchcock's prologues and wraparounds (all of which were penned by James Allardice) to ensure that "the series was an extension of [Hitchcock's] persona" (251).

Lane shrewdly identifies a key way in which Harrison used casting to create the sense that the series and Hitchcock's films were part of the same body of work: actors from his previous features, such as Joseph Cotten, Claude Rains,

Thelma Ritter, Hitchcock and Reville's daughter Patricia, Theresa Wright, Hume Croyn, and Joan Fontaine all appeared in various episodes, and the show also became a "proving ground for actors Hitchcock had contracted or may have been considering for future film projects" (260). These included Vera Miles, Martin Balsam (both of whom featured in *Psycho*, a film largely made with Hitchcock's TV, as opposed to regular film, crew), and Barbara Bel Geddes. Lane also reveals how Harrison used the show to help to support and bring back blacklisted (and "grey-listed") writers, actors, and directors, the most notable being actor and director Norman Lloyd (who also had a long history with Hitchcock, having appeared in *Saboteur* and *Spellbound*). She notes Harrison's bravery, observing that "someone in Joan's position attempting to break the blacklist—or even just bend it a bit was taking bold risk" (256). But for someone with Hitchcock's power it was easier. When Wasserman questioned the decision to employ Lloyd, all it took was for Hitchcock to reply "I want him." Lane argues that Harrison also made her own personal mark on the show, providing a "Harrison touch" and "playing a crucial historical role in importing film noir into television" (251). Harrison made a smooth and successful transition from the big to the small screen, and indeed the format played to her strengths and her preference for more intimate and character-driven stories. *Alfred Hitchcock Presents* and *The Alfred Hitchcock Hour* stand as the crowning achievements of her career.

Throughout Lane argues the case for Harrison as an exceptional, trailblazing woman. She emerges as a compelling character, taking bold steps to venture beyond her upbringing and parental expectations to throw her hat in with the Hitchcocks, and then leave them to strike out on her own in Hollywood. While she was undoubtedly aided by her looks, connections, and financially comfortable background, Harrison was also a highly independent and talented businesswoman and producer who forged her own path and was happy to shun a conventional lifestyle of marriage and children (she did not marry novelist Eric Ambler until she was 51).

While the book is a must-read for anyone interested in Hitchcock, it is also a rich and compelling read for its wider Hollywood history, including its accounts of women working in the film industry at this time managing to find their allies and endure their antagonists. The book creates a vivid picture of the cultural, political, and social scene during this period, from gatherings of European emigres such as Paul Henreid, Bertolt Brecht, Thomas Mann, and Igor Stravinsky, to Harrison's Saturday morning tennis at the Beverly Hills Tennis Club. The book sheds light on Harrison's response to the Hollywood blacklist, from lying low at times to boldly hiring talents whose careers had been put on hold. It also shows how television could offer a highly rewarding direction for film industry talents in the 1950s.

Throughout, the book benefits from first-hand accounts of Harrison and her world by friends and collaborators, such as those from Norman Lloyd, as well as Harrison's own voice as revealed through script notes, interviews, and guest columns. I enjoyed many of the details of Harrison's adjustment to life in Los Angeles and Lane's descriptions of the city and its society at the time, including Harrison's commissioning of Hungarian modernist architect Paul László to design her a house (the house became part of Harrison's publicity machine, and the book features several photographs showing the glamourous producer at work and repose there). As well as working hard, Harrison also played hard. Before her marriage to Ambler (who incidentally disliked Hitchcock immensely), she enjoyed many affairs, including relationships with Clark Gable, Billy Wilder, Sidney Bernstein, and others, as well as close friendships, which may have been romantic, with women such as writer Sarett Tobias. The book seamlessly blends the personal with the professional, as did Harrison herself, who worked with many of her paramours.

Phantom Lady: Hollywood Producer Joan Harrison, The Forgotten Woman Behind Hitchcock is impeccably researched and is both scholarly and a highly enjoyable read. It stands as a valuable addition to Hitchcock studies, expanding the ever-growing body of work on the importance of the director's collaborators. It supports recent research on the all-important figure of Alma Reville and makes the case that, as with Reville, Harrison's input was integral to Hitchcock's resulting films. Most crucially, though, *Phantom Lady* is a study of a woman whose impressive career in 1940s Hollywood has been overlooked up to this point. Through Christina Lane's book, Joan Harrison's life and work has now received fitting attention and recognition.

DIANE CARSON

Hitchcock's Shadow of a Doubt:
Social Critique and Cinematic Triumph

Diane Negra, *Shadow of a Doubt*. Liverpool: Auteur/Liverpool University Press, 2021. 140 pp. $90 cloth, $27.75 paperback.

In her book devoted entirely to director Alfred Hitchcock's 1943 film *Shadow of a Doubt*, Diane Negra makes a compelling case for her expansive, comprehensive scrutiny. As she points out early on, this is *the* film that, at various times, Hitchcock "identified as his favorite and his best," adding that "Paradoxically scholarly analysis of the film has been scant" (18). Though *Shadow* became Hitchcock's sixth American production, in his DVD extra "Beyond Doubt: The Making of Hitchcock's Favorite Film," Peter Bogdanovich contends that this is "really the first American Hitchcock," as it was his first film "made and set in America" (19). Negra thus initiates a solid introductory justification for the extensive inquiry that follows.

To remind both cinema scholars and film enthusiasts of the specifics of the story, Negra begins with a detailed, nine-page synopsis (8-16) that proves most helpful, informing her subsequent, rich evaluation. She then moves from "Hitchcock in America: *Shadow of a Doubt'*s Family Values" (18-23) to "A Note on Authorship" (24-25). Her description of the personal circumstances in Hitchcock's life during this WWII year provides valuable background that heightens our sense of the "psychological realism of *Shadow*" (19). Significantly, Hitchcock's mother Emma, still in England, died during the film's production and, because of the war, he could not return there. The mother in *Shadow* is also named Emma, and

Hitchcock's daughter Patricia was an adolescent at the time of the production of this film focusing principally on a young woman. Negra thereby places *Shadow* in the expatriate cinema tradition, and notes that Hitchcock's position as a newcomer to and outsider in America gave him a unique perspective from which to examine the "domestic thematics and staging of the family romance" (19). However, Negra clarifies that this will not be the primary focus for her study as she proceeds to a discussion primarily of the dynamics so "highly effective in building suspense and cultivating identification with characters" (20). While not the core of the subsequent chapters, the wartime context signals both Negra's inclusive (biographical) awareness and her critical diligence. Readers are put on notice that Negra has considered all relevant aspects of the production and has properly qualified their importance. This will include the ways both form and content interconnect, with elements from music and sound to formal structure to genre all complementing each other.

Before moving into those areas, in "A Note on Authorship" (24-25) Negra highlights the collaborative nature of film production, noting that "while regularly alluding to directorial authorship throughout this book, I am referring to a qualified authorship" (24), a vital stipulation too often excluded and, we'll see as the book unfolds, characteristic of Negra's discerning, multifaceted approach: on authorship and the credit Hitchcock should or should not receive, on his reputed misogyny, on multiple critics' interpretations of *Shadow,* and on the film's take on such highly charged subjects as the idealization of the family, pathologies of violence, psychoanalytic theories of human behavior, gender politics, and fascism.

Negra next expands her substantive inquiry in the section "Genre, Violence and Repression in *Shadow of a Doubt*" (26-36) with attention to "at least four fundamental generic registers": Pandora's Box Narrative, romance, wartime drama, and horror film. Here, as in all her other chapters, Negra quotes comprehensively from scholarly analyses of *Shadow.* If I have any criticism of this impressive work, it is that I would prefer fewer summaries and quotations from others. That is a minor quibble I hesitate to express, given that Negra uses her thorough knowledge of *Shadow* scholarship productively to inform and advance her own insights, at times challenging or qualifying previous works in convincing fashion. However, though her astute insights build persuasively to convincing assessments, copious quotations occasionally feel intrusive and unnecessary.

On balance and to her credit, when relevant, Negra introduces ideas from other, tangential academic fields. Regarding the family in *Shadow,* she applies Estella Tincknell's observations on "media representations of the familial" (26) and the pervasive idealization that Uncle Charles and young Charlie challenge. In that regard, as Tania Modleski argues and Negra concurs, Hitchcock expresses both misogyny and sympathy toward women, and is aware of and presents "the pathologies of violence" (27). In addressing the familiar debate around these irreconcilable polarities, Negra explores the vampire mythology reflected in *Shadow*'s art direction and in characters' numerous comments expressing the vampire trope. This fertile area yields engrossing revelations, highlighting threats to young Charlie, with Uncle Charles embodying often surprising, even unnerving horror. The vampiric intimations extend to the music, with Austro-Hungarian composer Franz Léhar's *Merry Widow March* calling to mind an unspecified but mysterious European ambiance often associated with vampires; Charles's objections to being photographed; backlit silhouettes; low-angle shots; and pertinent dialogue (for example, Graham telling Anne to "tell Catherine the story of Dracula"). Negra meticulously teases out the multiple explicit mentions of and implicit allusions to the vampire trope, and in the following sections ties its impact to her subsequent analysis of other aspects of the film.

Following this consideration of the vampire theme, Negra turns to a striking, central element: the "unlikely couple at its heart, Uncle Charles and his niece and namesake Charlie Newton [who] both cherish and despise the family" (31), their preternatural bonds and potentially incestuous connections alternating between mystifying and unsettling. In the wide-ranging discussion of this family resides a wealth of social critique, fully and thoughtfully interrogated in "The Family Romance in *Shadow of a Doubt*" (36-46). Here Negra integrates psychoanalytic theory to unpack additional facets of the narrative trajectory, contrasting idealism with disenchantment, underscoring the conflicted and contradictory reactions to Charles's and Charlie's meeting at the train, their betrothal scene in the kitchen, the shifting status of the ring that Uncle Charles gives to Charlie, and their emotional intimacy. The Charles/Charlie bond constitutes a provocative, thorny aspect of *Shadow*'s presentation of middle-class society in general and the Newton family in particular, a feature Negra probes, crediting it with the complexity it merits as superficial normality masks pathological underpinnings.

Negra pursues this complexity and the centrality of middle-class life in "Homesickness and *Shadow of a Doubt*" (46-54). Uncle Charles's insistence on the importance of home as a place of safety for himself intensifies the "emotionally complex relation to family" (46). Negra observes ways that Charles's comments foreground his desire for comfort with the profound tension inherent in families' restrictive environments: dependency alternating with repressed resentment. In this section, she also considers Ann's and Roger's normative gender roles along with Herb's and Joe's interest in homicide, revealing both their obliviousness to Charles's actions and their delight in and fascination with murder lore. Introducing several scholars' theoretical reflections on contemporary patriarchy, Negra places the film's multifaceted contemplation of domesticity squarely within the context of 1940s Hollywood cinema, a body of work that promotes a broad examination of American society.

Of equal importance Negra discusses Hitchcock's inclusion of an "extraordinary moment of empathy for a midlife woman" (52), crediting "Patricia Collinge's involvement in shaping the dialogue here that likely renders it so powerful and poignant." As part of a close study of the script compared to the finished film, Negra describes a scene written but omitted from the film, quoting original dialogue that would have added significant meaning, specifically Emma discounting her Newton family "in favor of the Oakleys" (53). Before concluding this section with a summary of the characters' familiar traditional roles, Negra identifies the significance of Charles's philanthropic gesture, bequeathing money at his death "for the children," hinting at a childhood trauma possibly triggering Charles's pathology.

Next, "Resonances of Film Noir and the Female Gothic in *Shadow of a Doubt*" (54-64), contextualizes 1940s cinema through an exploration of the female gothic that relies on "complex emotional and literal domestic geographies . . . activating themes of mistrust, suspicion and romantic disappointment" (55). This is a particularly fruitful topic given that the publicity for *Shadow*, illustrated by a poster reproduced in the text, pushed the association with gothic elements: female paranoia and passivity renounced; Charlie's discontent validated rather than repudiated; Charlie's competent detective work; and her recognition of Charles's violence and guilt. The typical conflation of love and violence, the unstable and unpredictable world, the film noir style, and the "morally troubled conclusion" set *Shadow* in the film noir world, with qualifications that Negra astutely describes.

"*Shadow of a Doubt* and Gendered Wartime Culture" (64-77) places this film definitively within its historical moment, even though, released in 1943, *Shadow* favors "oblique rather than direct references to a wartime context" (65). Production restrictions were wholly influenced by its moment, e.g., no night shooting and a $5,000 limit on set construction using new materials (78). Most interestingly, *Shadow's* ideological critique contrasts with the conventional mission of WWII films as directed by the Office of War Information: to provide reassurance to the home front. Several subtle, indirect references to the war notwithstanding, *Shadow* offers a subversive challenge to facile well-being. Negra furthers the analysis developed in previous sections by adding a fascinating textual connection to "fascist forms of domination and engagement" (69) evident in Charles's dinner speech and his overall pathology, perhaps connected to his apparent disqualification for military service. These fascist insinuations extend to gender politics, minority groups (though this film explicitly depicts only an oppressive white-on-white world), ageism (older widows being targeted), and struggle for authoritarian control "that often lurks beneath seemingly open social surfaces" (69). Restrictive gender representation contrasts with "female agency, capacity and resilience . . . key concerns of the wartime period" (71) and the issue Negra interrogates next: contemplating "Charlie as a girl detective" (71) who incites "pleasure and anxiety in the adult male" (72) because of her resourceful and effective investigative skill. Furthering the core complexity of her character, Charlie emerges as both contained within and fighting back against prescribed, restricted female identity.

"Santa Rosa as Site of Middle-Class Normalcy" (77-87) addresses the significance and impact of this particular California setting. Extending her earlier analysis, Negra probes the "broad lack of faith in the institutions and agencies that organize American life" (79), citing FBI agent Graham's ineptitude and mediocrity complemented by Santa Rosa's caricatured complacency, mercenary interests, and "socially problematic emotions" (79). The church, financial institutions, clubs, receptions, and the law are targets for mockery, insults, and derision. "Irresolution and Euthanasia in *Shadow of a Doubt*" (87-93) further scrutinizes the film's conclusion and the ineffectiveness of the law either to assuage concern or to reinforce optimism. After Charles's earlier suggestions of thoughts of suicide, his death, Negra proposes, is perhaps a mercy killing, "Charles essentially training Charlie in his methods" (90), an annihilation "essentially inevitable" (92). On this topic, Negra fittingly acknowledges that the internal evidence about Charles's death remains more elusive than definitive.

In "Domestic Space, Public Space and Transport in *Shadow of a Doubt*" (93-97), Negra looks at the film's thematic organization of locations and *mise-en-scène*. While every director makes important decisions in the staging of a film, too seldom does it receive the welcome attention Negra gives it. She notes that Hitchcock's carefully established contrast of public versus private, vertical versus horizontal, and personal versus shared spaces thematically conveys the "complex affinities and discrepancies" of the characters' interactions. Actions that take place at the telegraph office, the train station, the town square, the city library, the garage, doorways, and the house, especially the kitchen and the back stairs, reinforce emotional elements through their shot composition and design. Similarly, "the symbolics of transport and mobility" (96) express the politics of the gendered themes.

Moving to "*Shadow of a Doubt*'s Popular Culture Afterlife" (97-102), Negra offers a partial inventory of the film's impact as an inspiration and/or touchstone for other films, some productively examined in academic scholarship. While she includes related cinematic examples in earlier chapters (e.g., film noir, the female gothic), here she adds works with similarities and differences that offer promising avenues for further inquiry, some immediately obvious, others somewhat elusive yet highly intriguing, such as *The Silence of the Lambs, Blue Velvet, The Man Who Wasn't There, Scream*, serial killer fictions, and more.

Negra's "Conclusion" (103-09) summarizes her incisive investigation of *Shadow*'s "profound moral complexities and details" (105), revisiting the ending and finding anything but satisfaction in the final scene with Charlie and Graham outside the church where Charles's funeral is being held. The terrors embedded in *Shadow* persist after the "depiction of imperiled normality" (108) has concluded narratively and, again, we are left with an unforgettable impression of Charlie's disenchantment and the scene's staging. Thus, Negra's book is of great value in its insightful analysis of Hitchcock's presentation of the unresolved "engagement with the pathologies of violence in America" (109) and the placement of women within them, most significantly implicating the idealized family as not only a site but also a source of this violence. Through her encyclopedic, exceptionally thorough interrogation of these themes, with fifteen well-chosen frame grabs, four publicity stills, and two examples of contemporary press coverage effectively illustrating key points, Negra prompts appreciation of the breadth and depth of *Shadow of a Doubt* and implicitly encourages a further questioning of what has—or hasn't—changed in the America portrayed so dramatically, accurately, and ominously by Hitchcock.

DAVID GREVEN

Fragments and Fury

Bruce Isaacs. *The Art of Pure Cinema: Hitchcock and His Imitators*. New York: Oxford University Press, 2020. 272 pp. $39.95 paperback.

I have often considered my critical stance on Brian De Palma an anomalous one. While I consider Alfred Hitchcock the greatest of classical Hollywood directors (a placeholder description given his transatlantic career), I consider De Palma the greatest postclassical Hollywood director. Important critics of De Palma, such as Adrian Martin, Terrence Rafferty, Thomas Leitch, Pauline Kael, and especially Robin Wood, have defended his aesthetics, and specifically defended his work against the dread charge of "ripping-off Hitchcock," but not very many critics have written from a position of partisanship for both directors. (Kael famously angered Andrew Sarris and others by perversely proclaiming De Palma the infinitely greater director, but Eyal Peretz essentially follows suit in his book on De Palma, *Becoming Visionary: Brian De Palma's Cinematic Education of the Senses* [Stanford University Press, 2008].)

In *The Art of Pure Cinema*, Bruce Isaacs has, more than any other critic I have read, shed light on the peculiar and heady relationship between Hitchcock and De Palma, and in so doing has produced a thrilling account of De Palma's aesthetics that illustrates its singular force and overlaps with Hitchcock's. Isaacs also sheds revelatory light on Hitchcock, who, while not the sole focus of this book, is treated with ample rigor. Perhaps most thrillingly of all, Isaacs stages — and ably inspires — a bracing conversation among Hitchcock and several of his "imitators": De Palma and the *giallo* directors Dario Argento, Mario Bava, and Lucio Fulci. This is a book I have long waited for, and it exceeds my expectations in its finesse, rigor, insightfulness, and—most notable of all—committed demonstration of the art of close reading and textual analysis in this era of detachment and distance in Film Studies, characterized by what we can call archival hegemony.

Isaacs brilliantly breaks new ground by covering the seemingly well-covered terrain of Hitchcock's theory of "pure cinema." Excavating the meanings of this term, how Hitchcock got to it, and what it means for his cinema and its disciples is Isaacs's foundation. He points out that a desire to create "a cinema unaffiliated with earlier artistic forms" was not unique to Hitchcock but a goal shared by many early twentieth-century aesthetic modernists (15). "Pure cinema . . . was a European avant-garde movement that emerged during the mid-1920s in Paris," incorporating elements of German expressionism and Soviet montage and exemplified by the work of filmmakers Henri Chomette and Germaine Dulac (16).

The latter was particularly relevant to Hitchcock's early development as a film theorist, as was, of course, F.W. Murnau, the great German expressionist director whose filmmaking Hitchcock observed first-hand (*The Last Laugh*, 1924). Isaacs discusses connections between Murnau's and Dulac's views on pure cinema, which coalesced in Hitchcock's thought. Isaacs makes sure to clarify that Hitchcock did not take an active interest in Dulac's writings and films; instead, "his aesthetic development occurred in relative proximity to the emergence" of the pure cinema movement that Dulac led (18).

Isaacs contends that Hitchcock's cinema is one in which "narrative and representational form is increasingly distilled into the abstraction of cinema's pure formal and phenomenological elements: relations within space, movement, time (and thus duration), perception, affect, and intensity" (23). No wonder the *giallo* artists found his work so resonant! An early section of Isaacs's book includes a remarkably fresh and detailed look at the scene in *Frenzy*

(1972) when the murderer Rusk takes the deeply likable Babs, his unfortunate next victim, up the stairs to his flat, saying she is really "my type of woman," before Hitchcock's camera ominously backtracks into the street, where the ambient street noises slowly engulf the soundtrack. Isaacs painstakingly analyzes this sequence in order to demonstrate Hitchcock's negotiation, tethered to the impact of the tracking shot, of realist and anti-realist techniques, and he emphasizes a new excessiveness in the director's style, excess being a key linkage among Hitchcock and his adrenalized imitators (35).

As Isaacs points out, Hitchcock's films are "steadfastly anti-realist in their rejection of social and political realisms." (On a side note, I wonder if the reason that interesting late works like *Torn Curtain* [1966] and *Topaz* [1969] are routinely dismissed, if not denigrated altogether, is because their explicit Cold War context lets the social and political seams show?) Isaacs emphasizes that Hitchcock's "increasingly flamboyant" definitive works of the 1950s and 1960s defy Bazinian realism, Bazin's "image of the real . . . the capacity of the film image to communicate the ontological properties of reality" (37).

Italian genre cinema, specifically the *giallo*, reflects a "Hitchcockian stylistic legacy that emerges in relative proximity to the release of *Psycho*" (45). Made in the same year as that legendary film, Mario Bava's 1960 *Black Sunday* paved the way for the *giallo*'s emergence. Bava's *Blood and Black Lace* (1964) is widely recognized as the first "excessive *giallo*." Argento's films, from *The Bird with the Crystal Plumage* (1970) forward, foreground their Hitchcockian stylistic allegiances more explicitly. Fulci's *Don't Torture a Duckling* (1972) "represents one of the most flamboyant stylistic image and sound experiments" the *giallo* offers (47). Isaacs derives his view that the *giallo* should be understood as a "vernacular cinema" from the work of Mikel J. Koven. Hitchcock, *giallo*, and De Palma share a *"vernacular visuality"* (49; italics in the original).

Isaacs opines, "I suggest that De Palma's marginalization within the studio system is convincingly explained by his obsessive, highly specific, vernacular visual style and its concomitant lack of interest in classical narrative exposition, logical development, and plot resolution" (53). He proceeds from this premise to analyze the extraordinary two-shot of Malone (Sean Connery) and Ness (Kevin Costner) in *The Untouchables* (1987). The men talk in Chicago's Our Lady of the Sorrows church against the backdrop of the painted ceiling, which De Palma, using his trademark split diopter shot, films in a disorientingly woozy manner that defies the functionality of the dialogue, punctuated by Malone's question "What are you prepared to do?" The sequence represents "an entry into a deeper, reflexive meditation on visual cinematic form" (55).

Issacs expands his views of pure cinema through the theories of Eisenstein, Deleuze, and Bellour, focusing on the significance of "the part" and "the fragment." Using *Psycho's* famous or infamous shower scene as an example, the critic notes, "the part is always more than what is required of the articulation of the whole" (68). The radical attention that the part demands for itself, breaking from linear classical Hollywood storytelling, links the Hitchcock aesthetic to the *giallo*. Whereas even the transgressive Hitchcock adheres to certain traditional narrative and aesthetic stipulations, the *giallo* leads with "baroque, exhibitionistic excess," eschewing "the classicism of the whole for the fetishism of the part" (69). Isaacs understands De Palma's intertextual relationship to Hitchcock as always already mediated through *giallo* aesthetics. He reads the elevator murder sequence in De Palma's *Dressed to Kill* (1980), long viewed as a reworking of *Psycho's* shower murder, as exemplary of the director's *giallo* sensibility. (I devote a chapter to *Dressed to Kill* and De Palma's reworking of Hitchcock in my book *Psycho-Sexual: Male Desire in Hitchcock, De Palma, Scorsese, and Friedkin* [University of Texas Press, 2012].)

Isaacs offers several stunning close-reading set-pieces throughout, including one of the opening murder scene, rife with lurid color and astonishingly unexpected camera angles, in Bava's *A Bay of Blood* (1971). I do, however, take issue with Isaacs's reading of Hitchcock's use of the triple cut-in when focusing on Dan Fawcett's gouged-out eyes in *The Birds* (1963). The "jump cuts thoroughly distanciate the spectator from the action and from" the reaction of Lydia Brenner (Jessica Tandy). But for Isaacs, this "disjointed series of cuts covering action" "loses something of the affect of movement itself, and of the intensity of the fragment as part" (75). I think that the sequence fully achieves the "stunning intensity" that Isaacs oddly claims it "loses." For one thing, Hitchcock's emphasis on subjective camerawork, through which we identify with the person seeing and their emotions, dominates here. The repressed, and repressive, Lydia both wants to see what has happened and does not want to see, to register reality and deny it, an ambivalent stance she painfully maintains throughout the film. The triple cut-in, reminiscent of the famous *Vertigo* dolly-in, zoom-out effect, registers Lydia's emotional state, the harrowing push-pull experience of wanting and not wanting to know, and of finally being overwhelmed, indeed crushed, by knowledge. (Isaacs makes no mention of what Robin Wood described as the "beautiful/ugly" shot of the dead bird caught in the partially shattered window.)

For the most part, however, Isaacs does what, in my view, is the primary task of the critic, to explain and contemplate the power of the work of art, and the implications of an artist's work. Film Studies of the present time focuses on production history and ideological ramifications of works, trends, and platforms. But Isaacs does what critics like Wood, Durgnat, Cavell, Marian Keane, and William Rothman have done: present the work in its fullness, so that the appreciative appraisal draws from and flows out of the full-bodied evocation of the work. Isaac moves toward a superb Conclusion that deftly recapitulates his main arguments and offers a stunning close reading of De Palma's masterpiece (hopefully not his last), *Femme Fatale* (2002), which Isaacs enhances, as he does throughout the book, with stunning color stills linked to his unpacking of De Palma's film aesthetics. I have not yet come across as detailed, finely honed, and precise a close reading of De Palma's "segmented" cinema. And that it is joined by exhaustive and detailed readings of Hitchcock and the high points of the *giallo* tradition makes this exhilarating, densely and daringly argued work a must-read.

Contributors

John Bruns is Professor of English and Director of Film Studies at the College of Charleston. He holds a Ph.D. in Film, Literature, and Culture from the University of Southern California. He is the author of *Hitchcock's People, Places, and Things* (Northwestern University Press, 2019). He has published essays in *Film Criticism, Hitchcock Annual, Journal of Narrative Theory, New Review of Film and Television Studies,* and *Texas Studies in Literature & Language.* Most recently, he coauthored a film history textbook with Charles Ramírez Berg.

Diane Carson is professor emerita at St. Louis Community College, Past-President of the University Film and Video Association, and contributes weekly film reviews to KDHX (88.1) FM and the Alliance of Women Film Journalists. She has published articles in recent anthologies on Preston Sturges, John Barrymore, and Clint Eastwood, and cowritten/coedited books on acting, John Sayles, and food in film. She has co-directed two documentaries: *Other People's Footage: Copyright & Fair Use* and *Other People's Footage: Fair Use in Scripted Films* (both 2019).

Sidney Gottlieb is Professor Communication and Media Studies at Sacred Heart University, Fairfield, Connecticut. He has edited (with Donal Martin) and contributed to *Haunted by* Vertigo: *Hitchcock's Masterpiece Then and Now,* a collection of essays from a variety of Hitchcock scholars, forthcoming from John Libbey/Indiana University Press. He is currently editing a volume of interviews with Hirokazu Kore-eda for the University Press of Mississippi series Conversations with Filmmakers.

David Greven is Professor of English at the University of South Carolina. He publishes in the fields of nineteenth-century American literature and Film Studies. His books include *Intimate Violence: Hitchcock, Sex, and Queer Theory* (Oxford University Press, 2017), *Queering the Terminator* (Bloomsbury, 2017), *Ghost*

Faces: Hollywood and Post-Millennial Masculinity (SUNY Press, 2016), *Psycho-Sexual* (Texas University Press, 2012), and *Representations of Femininity in American Genre Cinema* (Palgrave, 2011). He is currently writing a book on the Merchant-Ivory film *Maurice* (1987) for the revived *Queer Film Classics* series edited by Thomas Waugh and Matthew Hays.

Thomas Leitch, Profesor of English at the University of Delaware, is the author of *Find the Director and Other Hitchcock Games* and *The Encyclopedia of Alfred Hitchcock* and coeditor, with Leland Poague, of *A Companion to Alfred Hitchcock*. His most recent book is *The History of American Literature on Film*.

Henry K. Miller is a researcher at the University of Reading, working on the archive of Stephen Dwoskin. In 2014 he edited *The Essential Raymond Durgnat* for BFI/Palgrave Macmillan, having earlier written the foreword to the second edition of Durgnat's last book, *A Long Hard Look at 'Psycho.'* He is the author of *The First True Hitchcock*, forthcoming in 2022 from University of California Press

Nathalie Morris is a film historian, writer, and curator. She has previously written about Alma Reville and her contribution to Hitchcock's films. In 2012 she curated the exhibition "Hitchcock's Britain," and also made a short film in which she cooked Hitchcock's Quiche Lorraine on camera, as part of the major British Film Institute project, "39 Steps to the Genius of Hitchcock." She is currently Collections Curator at the Academy Museum in Los Angeles.

David Sterritt is editor in chief of *Quarterly Review of Film and Video*, contributing writer at *Cineaste*, film professor at the Maryland Institute College of Art, former chair of the National Society of Film Critics and the New York Film Critics Circle, and author or editor of fifteen books including *The Films of Alfred Hitchcock* and *Simply Hitchcock*. He has lectured on Hitchcock at the National Gallery of Art, the Boston

Museum of Fine Arts, the Brooklyn Museum, and the Motion Picture Association of America, and his writing on Hitchcock has appeared in many journals and edited collections.

Michael P. Walker is a retired teacher. He has contributed articles to *Movie* magazine, *Movie: A Journal of Film Criticism*, *Framework*, *Film Dope*, *CineAction*, and *Hitchcock Annual*, and to the *The Movie Book of Film Noir* (1992), *The Movie Book of the Western* (1996), *Alfred Hitchcock: Centenary Essays* (1999), *Style & Meaning: Studies in the Detailed Analysis of Film* (2005), *A Companion to Stephen Spielberg* (2017) and *The Call of the Heart: John M. Stahl and Hollywood Melodrama* (2018). His books are *Hitchcock's Motifs* (2005), *Modern Ghost Melodramas: What Lies Beneath* (2017), and *Endings in the Cinema: Thresholds, Water and the Beach* (2020). His current project, *Persecuted Wives: The Hollywood Female Gothic Film of the 1940s*, will be published later this year as an e-book.